Approaching sociology

Approaching sociology

Margaret A. Coulson
and
Carol Riddell

Routledge & Kegan Paul
London, Boston and Henley

First published in 1970
Second edition 1980
by Routledge & Kegan Paul Ltd
39 Store Street, London WC1E 7DD,
9 Park Street, Boston, Mass. 02108, USA and
Broadway House, Newtown Road,
Henley-on-Thames, Oxon RG9 1EN
Set in IBM Press Roman by
Hope Services, Abingdon, Oxon
and printed in Great Britain by
Lowe & Brydone Ltd
Thetford, Norfolk

British Library Cataloguing in Publication Data

Coulson, Margaret Anne
Approaching sociology. – 2nd ed.
1. Sociology
I. Title II. Riddell, Carol
301   HM51   80–40535

ISBN 0 7100 0574 1
ISBN 0 7100 0575 X Pbk

Contents

Introduction to the second edition

When we first wrote this book

We wrote the first version of this book at the end of the 1960s. It was a period of political and social criticism, creativity and optimism in many parts of the world. In late capitalist countries, like Britain, there were large protest movements against the American war in Vietnam. Radical and revolutionary students criticized their courses, their teachers and the conservatism of educational institutions in capitalist societies. Workers began to use more imaginative forms of struggle such as factory occupations and flying pickets. Black people and third world immigrants developed movements for their civil rights, out of which grew attempts to redefine the experience of being Black or Asian. In the north of Ireland, the civil rights movement and the violent response to it upset an appearance of political calm which had become taken for granted in Britain. The Czech people's attempts for change found an even more violent response. After decades of silence about women's subordination and oppression, the women's movement emerged again, and a new wave of sexual politics challenged the split between public and personal life. Culturally, movements like that of the hippies disdained the glittering consumer society and some of its sexual repressions. Even commercially produced popular music was more exuberant, rebellious and optimistic. The apparent consensus of the politics of the 1950s was in a state of collapse.

At the same time, the post Second World War economic boom was on the decline. In the rarefied academic world of sociology, things were in a mess, a mess which reflected the ideological and political crises of the world outside. In the 1950s and early 1960s, many sociologists in established positions in the USA and to a lesser extent in Britain had worked to establish the academic and professional status of sociology and its 'usefulness' to governments, business and other establishment bodies and sources of funding. By taking controversy out of sociology, they hoped to demonstrate the 'scientific' nature of sociological methods of counting and quantifying, claiming to be able to turn the social world into statistical categories and formulae. Functionalism was the dominant theoretical approach of establishment sociology.

By the end of the 1960s, such a sociology looked pretty hopeless to growing numbers of students who had expected to find in it some clues to understanding the social world. On the other hand, governments and industry had allowed sociology to expand into more and more educational and other institutions. It became part of professional training for social workers, teachers and other groups. This was the context in which we wrote *Approaching Sociology*. We wrote as teachers of sociology, frustrated with most introductory texts which didn't seem to have much connection (even less critical connection) with the social world. We tried to build into our approach ways of criticizing sociology and sociologists themselves, and of seeing the subject in a wider context. Over the past decade there has been an enormous increase in critical social science studies. Within academic sociology, arguments have shifted somewhat away from functionalism to a preoccupation with the social dimensions of people's face-to-face interactions and perceptions.

What we've changed

The revisions we have made for this second edition have not altered the main outline of the book. Many introductory and applied courses have not changed very greatly; there, functionalism is certainly not dead, many awkward controversies and problems are still ignored, and our arguments in relation to these issues are still relevant. We have ironed out some of the pretentiousness of the first edition, and tried to make what we have written more intelligible to people who are beginning sociology. The growth of the feminist movement has made us more sensitive to the sexist assumptions of everyday sociological work (the study of 'man in society'), and of everyday life. We have tried to challenge those assumptions in the way in which we have written. We have updated references, added some new examples and extended others. We have given more attention to theories of interaction, labelling, ethno-methodology and the 'management of appearances', criticizing the extent to which these have reflected a retreat from larger issues of social structures — relationships of power and inequality.

The changing context

As the 1980s begin, the social climate is very different from a decade ago. The political and economic crisis which has been developing through that period is tightening around us. This is reflected in and against the social sciences. As the state gives priority to defence and law and order at the expense of education, health and welfare services, so the social sciences, especially perhaps sociology, lose their appeal to the establishment. Sociology is being eased out of many areas of training, the number of undergraduate and research students is being reduced. It is no longer so useful to those in control.

Academic sociology certainly does not tell us how to save the world from disaster, how to resolve the present crisis, how to transform society into something more humane and creative. But it can't be allowed to obscure and deny the existence of controversy and argument and conflict of interests in the social world.

Within sociology now, there is a professional law and order brigade anxious to police the subject back into a safe conformism, reclaiming sociology as a totally conservative discipline, outlawing radical, critical work. We hope that that project will fail. By actually studying people and societies, we are always liable to disturb a consensus sociology, and reveal that there are conflicts of interest and aspiration which are central to social life in the societies we know.

MARGARET COULSON
CAROL RIDDELL

Chapter one

Sociology as a critical discipline

The diversity of views in sociology

All over the world, people starting to learn about physics, or any other of the natural sciences, will be learning very much the same sort of things. The same sets of basic propositions will be learnt in Japan and Russia, China and Peru. But this is not true in sociology. The student in Russia will not start off with the same propositions about societies and people's relation to them as the student in the USA. The British student and the Yugoslav student will not be learning the same sorts of propositions to start off their studies (Aron, 1968, pp. 7f.). More than this, even within a country, to a considerable extent the approach which students find they are being taught varies according to the particular views of their teachers or departments. In Canada, for example, two distinct traditions of sociology exist side by side: French Canadian, drawing from European and especially French sociology, and English Canadian, which follows one or other of the American schools (Bottomore, 1969, pp. 112–13). In some places the diversity of views on the subject will be emphasized, in others it will be ignored, or underplayed. No doubt there will be some elements in common in most of the courses students will be taking across the world, but these will, in fact, be very largely restricted to the study of such things as technical means of carrying out surveys of opinion and attitude, around which a certain amount of technology has developed. Among sociologists there are different reactions to the problem of the diversity of approaches and orientations. It will tell us something of what sociology is about if we examine them.

For some sociologists, the problem is relatively simple. Since *their* approach is right, and those of other schools wrong, the latter can safely be ignored. It is very easy to see this if we compare basic textbooks of sociology from different countries — the kind of contents that they list, the kind of authors they consider important, the kind of orientations that they adopt. Here are some examples. There are large numbers of American textbooks, well-produced, very lengthy (in no country are there so many students of sociology as there are in the USA). Almost all of them orient their approach to sociology around the concept of *culture*, which we shall discuss later. But if we look at European textbooks, we find them giving much less emphasis to the idea of culture, and emphasizing much more the idea of *structure*. Similarly, in most American, and in a number of British textbooks, the idea of social change is given a very subordinate place — sometimes a chapter is 'tacked on' to a book — whereas all East European textbooks give a central place to the concept of change. George Gurvitch, one of the great French sociologists (although we do not agree with his sociological approach in general), calls Marx the 'Prince of Sociologists', and Marx's work is basic to the approach of large numbers of East European sociologists; yet he is not even given the dignity of a section in Barnes's 1000-page *Introduction to the History of Sociology*, and hardly, if at all, mentioned in most of the American introductory texts (Barnes, 1966). While most of the latter depend almost entirely on the *functionalist* orientation to sociology, in Bottomore's textbook, which is a widely used textbook in Britain, this orientation is dismissed in a few lines (Bottomore, 1969). Yet, if one's reading were confined to the approach of one of the particular schools mentioned, one would hardly even know that other approaches existed, and were widely held elsewhere. We think it is unfortunate that this applies to very many students of the subject, whose orientation is implicitly selected for them before they begin.

A comparison of an American and a Yugoslav textbook of sociology
A

Leonard Broom and Philip Selznick, *Sociology*, 3rd edition, 1973	Ante Fiamengo, *Elements of General Sociology*, 5th edition, 1967
Part I Elements of Sociological Analysis	Introduction

Quite a difference! Notice that even from the chapter headings you can see that Broom and Selznick's emphasis is static, while Fiamengo's is dynamic; Fiamengo's structuralist, while B. and S. emphasize culture and socialization. We should say that a comparison of the total contents of the two books bear out the differences in the contents' lists.

Another justification of the limitations which authors impose on the knowledge they presume to allow students of sociology is that the 'theoretical' problems are too difficult for beginning students to grasp; they need a firm base before they can tackle these more difficult questions. This would be acceptable, perhaps, if there was indeed a 'firm base', which had been solidly established, examples have already been given to indicate that this is not the case. The argument is therefore spurious.

An alternative approach, again popular in American textbooks, is to argue that sociology is a science, just like the natural sciences, but at a much less developed level; therefore evaluations and controversy should be avoided in the introductory stages. If, however, we examine these books in a comparative way, we find that, although sociology clearly is undeveloped when compared with the natural sciences in terms of the amount of effort, resources, and time given to research, what *has* been done has not led to a body of agreement which we can be sure that everybody accepts. While sociologists will not dispute that x per cent of people have a particular opinion on some subject at a particular time when asked a certain question, what this *means* in terms of their behaviour, in terms of theories about the explanation of behaviour in society, *will* be in dispute (see chapter 6). In addition to this, the proponents of such a view are unable to match up to the scientific criteria they set themselves. For example, in Horton and Hunt's *Sociology* (1976), the first chapter tells us about the scientific nature of sociology, that it abjures value judgments, unverifiable and unsubstantiated statements, etc., yet the authors find themselves able later on to describe the Soviet Union as an 'unparalleled tyranny'. Inkeles, in *What is Sociology?* (1964), after similar obeisance to the god of Science, concludes his book with a section which reads: 'The United States is viewed by most peoples of the world as dynamic and progressive to a degree which they hardly can imagine, and certainly do not expect to realize, for their own countries' (p. 112). Over and above this, the scientific methods used, despite their apparent sophistication, are often inappropriate to the problems.

The argument so far leads up to the proposition that we should regard with considerable distrust anyone who tries to tell us that there is *an* approach to sociology which we should learn alone, that there is *really* a considerable amount of agreement about most things, so that we needn't bother about the argument. The effect is to lull the critical faculties of students — who often find it difficult enough to cope with the amount of new knowledge anyway — and to make it easier for teachers to put across their approaches, or that of their school of sociology, without challenge. It can be confidently asserted that the interpretation of almost any piece of social evidence is controversial as between different sociological schools. No approach to the study of sociology which does not emphasize this fact should be acceptable. A second important line of argument follows from the first. Since there is no agreed base, from the beginning sociology students have to make judgments about, and interpretations of, the various propositions that they are introduced to. It is impossible to make such judgments on an *ad hoc* basis, and it is essential to have some kind of broader theoretical perspective which integrates material, and provides criteria by which to evaluate problems. In our view, the choice of such a perspective is not something arbitrary — tweedledum or tweedledee — but develops as a student relates different approaches to different problems and implicitly compares them. Nor should a perspective or approach be held in an absolute manner — or we should be dealing with a theology, not a social science. Yet many introductory textbooks ignore the need to inform students of the perspectives available for them to choose from. Instead we are given selections from a range of the various areas that sociologists have studied — urban sociology, industrial sociology, sociology of crime and delinquency, sociology of education, socialization, and so on; selections which are made on the basis of the perspectives of the author, who nowhere gives the student the opportunity to judge these perspectives themselves by laying them out in contrast to those of other sociologists. Again the big American textbooks are most guilty on this score, but some of the British ones are almost equally bad (e.g. Cotgrove, 1975, who indicates some of the problems in his first chapter, without apparently realizing their fundamental importance). We have our own views as to the most appropriate sort of perspective for sociologists, and put it forward in this book, because we think that an introductory book ought to do this. We also try to introduce some other perspectives critically, and give references so that students may, by additional reading, make judgments as to their relative helpfulness.

Sociologists as people

There are therefore very big disagreements among sociologists about orientations to the subject, and about the attitude that should be taken to the disagreements themselves. Why is this? It is in part due to differences of assessment of certain theories and actual studies, and it is with argument about these that the later parts of the book are concerned, but the problem is itself also a sociological one. Sociologists, and, to a greater or lesser degree, other social scientists, face two important kinds of problems in their work. First in the propositions that they make about people — how they are affected by belonging to certain kinds of groups, indeed, more than this, that people are inconceivable without groups. Mannheim, a famous sociologist, put it thus:

> We belong to a group not only because we are born into it, not merely because we confess to belong to it, nor finally because we give it our loyalty and allegiance, but primarily because we see the world and certain things in the world the way it does (Mannheim, 1966, p. 19).

But sociologists are also people, are therefore also members of groups, and, in as far as the above statement is true, will also tend to see the world in the way the groups they belong to do. Therefore we should expect to learn something about what sociologists say as sociologists by studying the nature of the different kinds of groups they belong to. (We are using the word group in a very general sense here, and not simply thinking of people meeting together face to face.)

There has been some objection to this kind of approach on the grounds that it lands one in what is called an infinite regression — people making the analysis of the effect on sociologists of being in groups themselves belong to groups; thus their analysis could itself be analysed in the same terms, and so on ad infinitum. Philosophically, the point is true, but, in practice, the possibility of an infinite regression does not allow us to ignore the problem. Some studies in social psychology have shown that, even under apparently very careful designs, the attitudes and expectations of the investigators have marked effects on the results (Rosenthal, 1967). Why then should the problem be ignored in sociology, or indeed in real life, where such rigour of experiment can, for various reasons, never hold?

The second problem for sociologists is that their subject matter is inextricably bound up with the kinds of problems whose solution concerns every human being in one way or another; over which vast, continent-wide disagreements exist; for which many have died — such problems as war and peace; capitalism and socialism; poverty and wealth; race relations; the relations between men and women; and so on. To investigate them involves sociologists in great historical arguments, and makes it very difficult for them to divorce their own views as citizens from their work as sociologists. Some sociologists have tried to evade this problem by resolutely refusing to study anything that might conceivably have social significance (cf. Moore, 1963). But this is really no escape, since even the decision as to what to study or what not to study is a social decision: 'By their work, all students of man and society assume and imply moral and political decisions' (Mills, 1970, p. 76). To a greater or lesser degree, in various ways, sociologists cannot avoid the problem of social values in their work. We do not think that the first and second problems are totally separable, since one of our basic propositions is that values and ideas are not independent of the groups, and relations between groups in which people find themselves, although this doesn't mean that they are considered to be totally determined by them. The problem is analysed further in chapter 5.

On the basis of these two related problems for sociologists, let us therefore return to the fact that there is no basic agreement among sociologists in different societies with different social structures, and even within societies, and that they so often try to hide or play down or 'leave until later' this uncomfortable fact. We can pose it this way: what are some of the characteristics of the sorts of groups that socio- logists belong to? (Cf. Horowitz, 1968.) Since this is a general socio- logical question, it applies to more groups than sociologists alone, so in our discussion we shall be raising propositions which can help us to understand how sociology should approach the study of other social problems. Because our discussion is not intended as a systematic analysis of the 'sociology of sociologists', it is phrased in very general terms, and will not enable us to predict the behaviour of individual sociologists (see below, p. 11).

Let us start off at a very general level, that of whole societies. Those groups who have effective control of a society may propose that only certain forms of approach or theory are proper, and may be prepared to enforce their view with violence or threats to the security of the sociologist. Thus, in fascist Germany, sociologists were required to work within a framework of racialist myths so intolerable that most of them felt obliged to leave (Neumann, 1967). Antonio Gramsci, a lead- ing Italian thinker, spent ten years of his life in the jail where he eventually died (Merrington, 1968). For many years, sociology was not an acceptable discipline in the Soviet Union, and at the time of writing the works of one of the critical Soviet social analysts, Leon Trotsky, are not available to students there.

There may be more subtle means of control. In the USA, an enquiry in 1955 by Lazarsfeld and Thielens, conducted on a sample of nearly 2,500 social science teachers, found that very nearly one quarter censored their own teaching so as to avoid difficulties, and 40 per cent were concerned lest 'warped' versions of what they said were passed on by students. More than two thirds of those in the bigger institutions of high academic repute knew of at least one incident involving attacks on colleagues for their views or associations (Lazarsfeld and Thielens, 1955). Thus, strong pressures may be exerted by those controlling societies, in some cases more directly, in some cases in a more

7

roundabout way, for sociology to be taught in a certain way, for some approaches to be emphasized at the expense of others (Birnbaum, 1958). If we continue to consider the USA, and we wish to do so, since the influence of its sociology is a dominant one in Britain, the development of teaching in sociology since the Second World War cannot be divorced from the confrontation between that country (and its allies) and the Soviet Union (and its allies). While it would be a crude over-simplification to say that the popularity of theories emphasizing order, stability, and the maintenance of the status quo (functionalism), was a result of a demand for an ideology to provide a weapon in the struggle against Soviet 'socialism', it would be even more crudely mistaken to believe that this type of theory developed entirely as a result of independent reflection (Aron, 1968, introduction, Cohn-Bendit, 1969).

Coercion and pressure are, then, more or less important to sociologists in different societies at different historical periods. But what of the students of teachers who practise self-censorship in one form or another? What was deliberate distortion on their part will appear a natural approach to the students who, when they begin to influence others, will not be censoring themselves in expressing censored views — they don't know that biases are incorporated in their approach. It may be objected that the teaching of sociology is not a simple matter of passing on information (or lack of it) from one generation to the next, that there are other influences. This is true, but let us suppose that most of these other influences tend to work in the same way; in that case the biases presented by the original teachers would be reinforced. Thus, if we call all the factors together going to make new sociologists, their *socialization*, and if all those factors reinforce a similar bias, then that bias isn't seen as a bias, but as the obvious, sensible, reasonable, scientific approach. This is one way in which schools of sociology, and social ideologies in general, are developed.

Let us consider therefore some of the other factors. There is a famous study by Bettleheim of the behaviour of the inmates of a Nazi concentration camp (Bettleheim, 1943). So adaptable are human beings that many prisoners, under the extreme pressure of the life in the camp, came to believe that they really were the despicable scum of the earth that the guards thought they were. In sociological jargon, they internalized the standards of the guards about themselves. Sociologists are not subject to such extreme pressures; but neither is what may be demanded of them so serious in its implications for their self-esteem. Thus for every sociologist who used self-censorship in the US enquiry referred to, we can be sure that there were others, many others, who

8

did not need self-censorship, because nothing that they said would be likely to disturb anyone – they had come to define sociology in terms which would not cause trouble. If we generalize this point to other situations, and indeed to whole societies, as Marcuse has quite legitimately done, it creates immense problems in defining what people's *real* beliefs are, problems discussed in chapter 5 (Marcuse, 1972).

We have talked about pressures on sociologists to teach in certain ways, emphasize certain approaches to the exclusion of others, and about how these are transmitted – either by coercion, internalization, or adoption over generations (of sociologists). It is also important that groups of people in some types of occupations differ in their attitudes, and in their standard and mode of life from those in other types. The explanation of these differences is a crucial question for sociology – all too often they are just described. In our class societies, sociologists are very definitely middle class. Let us consider the British situation. Established sociology teachers in university or college move in a restricted and comfortable world. Until recently their employment has been secure, and still is in the university sector. They are well paid, with steady rises in income apart from certain minor anxiety periods at job changes – until retirement, or near it. They have rather comfortable working conditions, long holidays, and comfortable houses in the suburbs of fairly large urban centres. The source of income for all this is the state, and, as Niclaus (1978) points out, there is a price to be paid for such support. Of course, not only sociologists, but all college and university teachers are in more or less this position, and their social attitudes are likely to reflect it. Those with a conscience tend to wish everyone could live like them, and the others worry about groups which might conceivably be a threat to them in some way or another as student militants seemed at the end of the 1960s. Such a background, the atmosphere and associations deriving from it, tend to make certain kinds of social theory seem more appropriate than others. Certain standards of politesse develop – norms of appropriate behaviour in the jargon – which lead to some types of argument being disparaged because of the 'rough' language in which they are expressed, their polemical style, or because of their author's 'dubious' connections, rather than because of their content (e.g. Lipset and Smelser, 1961, footnote 12).

In the USA, where job security has always been less certain until the higher reaches of the academic world, pressure to conform to certain norms is reinforced by the local power wielded by those in a position to confirm or deny appointments, a situation which has been ably studied by Caplow and McGhee in their book *The Academic Marketplace* (1961). Current government cutbacks in education leading to redundancies in polytechnics and colleges and an overall shortage of teaching jobs for sociologists have reduced job security in Britain. One effect of this has been to produce a greater insistence and commitment to a safe conformity in established ideas as the surest way to get a job, to keep it or to get promotion. Teachers resistant to such pressures have been more openly attacked. Sociologists, as academics, face clear pressures to behave as academics 'should'.

Pressures also develop among the sociologists themselves. Sociologists, in this country at least, have only recently and tentatively arrived at positions of academic respectability in the eyes of their longer established colleagues. They are often like *nouveaux riches*, trying to establish the power of their departments, and their status in academic institutions. This situation leads to an emphasis on the 'real' unity of the discipline, the *consensus* (amount of agreement as to norms) of the discipline, the professional qualities of sociologists, and their ability to make 'positive' contributions to the administration of things as they are. It leads away from an emphasis on disagreement, and theories which argue that problems derive from the fact that things are as they are, i.e., that the social organization itself needs changing if the problems are to be solved. There is also a tendency for sociologists to become so absorbed in establishing themselves professionally in the eyes of other sociologists whom they look up to (their *reference groups*), that the relationship between what they do and social reality can become very tenuous indeed. Some of the arguments about sociological arguments seem to us to have a very great resemblance to the medieval disputations as to the number of angels that could be accommodated on the head of a pin. Compare, for instance, Hoselitz and Moore (1966), Sosensky (1964), Zollschan and Perucci (1964) with the devastating critique by Frank (1971).

What we have done is to set out some of the pressures that we can expect to be exerted upon sociologists as teachers because of the fact that they are members of certain groups, and how these pressures may be reinforced through time. Let us summarize them. By belonging to a society with a certain type of social structure (e.g. capitalist, communist), they may be *coerced* in certain ways. More subtle pressures may lead them to *adapt* themselves by adopting as their own, *internalizing*, the demands made upon them. Succeeding generations may be so *socialized* that they will be less aware that choices are available. Within the society, because of their membership of certain occupational groups, sociologists are constantly pressured to approach their studies from the perspective of these groups; by adopting current *norms* giving high values to personal social advancement, for example, they are pressured not to behave in ways which might offend those in positions above them in order to secure their own advancement, and to ensure support for their research. Finally, by belonging to a local academic group of sociologists, they are pressured to adjust themselves to that which will gain them prestige in the eyes of the majority of that group − or the opinion formers, the influentials, within it.

This, then, is a general sociological approach by which we can begin to explain why whole schools of sociologists systematically misinform their students as to the extent of the diversity of approaches that exist within sociology. It is sociological, because it tries to relate behaviour and attitudes to the kinds of social groups that sociologists belong to. The same *kind* of analysis is a basis for the sociological study of all behaviour and attitudes, i.e., it tells us the sorts of questions that sociologists should ask when approaching social problems. If you want to understand your own behaviour and ideas, this is the way as a sociologist you could begin to approach it. You will find this type of analysis in all the examples that we give. Two further points should be mentioned.

First, this kind of approach does not tell us that every sociologist subject to similar influences will behave in the same way − such a crude determinism has been very frequent in social theories. It leads to endless struggling as the theorists seek to escape self-made problems, since people don't always behave as they 'ought to'. It helps us to understand types of behaviour which generally exist among groups of people who call themselves sociologists, and no more than this. The other point is related to the first. Since no narrow determinism is involved, sociologists who become aware that these pressures are affecting their approaches can, if they wish, alter the situation somewhat − either by changing the group affiliations that they have, or by trying to compensate for their group affiliations. Strong criticism from students can modify teachers' behaviour as well. We think that the purpose of sociology is not to build a closed system of determinate laws but, by informed study, to enable people to become aware of some of the social reasons for the social problems that they experience, and to be able to direct their attention to appropriate sorts of remedies for them. It can also help them to understand themselves better.

Our criticisms of the way sociologists often teach are not meant to be attacks on the value of studying the subject of sociology, but are

11

part of an argument as to why even first year students need a critical approach to what they are taught.

> If we would teach students how science is made, really made rather than as publicly reported, we cannot fail to expose them to the whole scientist by whom it is made, with all his gifts and blindnesses, with all his methods as well. To do otherwise is to usher in an era of spiritless technicians who will be no less lacking in understanding than they are in passion, and who will be useful only because they can be used (Gouldner, 1963).

Society

One of the 'groups' that we talked of in discussing the problem of sociologists and their subject was society. It is worth having a further look at this term, and terms related to it, because they have been, and are, the source of endless confusion among sociologists and others. Sociologists are always talking about society, but very few of them bother to define it satisfactorily. In some of the huge 'scientific' American textbooks of the subject, there is no definition at all.

In common usage, 'society' can refer to a small group formed for some purpose — a learned society, a student political society, and so on — but sociologists don't use it in this meaning. The term is also sometimes used in a very vague and general sense to denote a huge region with some common cultural or organizational feature — e.g. 'Western society'. But usually we mean a nation state when we talk of a society. If we talk about Indian society, or Zulu society, or British society, we are referring to the whole collection of things, people and goings-on within the boundaries of India, Zululand or Britain. There are two problems with this everyday use of the term society. First, it is all right to explain the behaviour of someone in terms of the pressures caused by being a member of a society organized in a certain way, but it is quite wrong to say that the society caused the behaviour. It is very tempting to do this, as a sort of shorthand, but the result is an impression that there is an odd sort of thing — society — over and above the individuals and things, and their organization, in a nation. This seems silly enough when presented in this way, and is called the error of *agelicism* or *reification* — treating as an object something which is not an object (Berger and Pullberg, 1966; Blackburn, 1969, pp. 206f.). Nevertheless, it is very common, and some famous sociologists (notably

Émile Durkheim) often give the impression that some mystical entity, society itself, is a cause of people's behaviour (Benoit-Smullyan, 1966). In justification, Durkheim was arguing against people who said that being in a society had no influence on people's behaviour. Here are some examples from sociology books to show how this 'shorthand' can confuse things:

Often society becomes the *initiator* rather than the *location* of some activity or pattern of organization: 'Every society controls to some extent who may mate with whom' (Goode, 1964). The more the idea is developed, the more confusing it becomes. For example, Berger (1970, p. 112) compares the relationship between individual and society to that between actor and playwright:

> We can say that society provides the script for all the dramatis personae. The individual actors, therefore, need but slip into the roles already assigned to them before the curtain goes up. As long as they play their roles as provided for in the script the social play can proceed as planned.

So 'society' 'plans', 'writes' and 'assigns' the parts we play! The metaphor may be introduced to emphasize the importance of social influences on our behaviour, but this personification of society prevents us from developing an understanding of the actual sources of these influences or of their interplay; everything is masked by what 'society' does or says. This criticism is developed further on page 28.

Inkeles (1964, p. 35) describes the main concern of one of the influential schools of sociologists, the structural functionalists, as being an attempt:

> to delineate the conditions and demands of social life, and to trace the process whereby a given society arranges to meet its needs. To choose an obvious example, if a society is to continue, it must periodically find new members. In all known societies the need is met by some form of family system. The family is the institution which 'acts' for society to ensure fulfillment of the functions of sexual reproduction, of early care of the dependent infant, and of his initial training in the ways of the society in which he will live.

Perhaps this rather bizarre picture of 'society' periodically noticing that it needs some new recruits and setting up families to produce and

13

mould these to the appropriate specifications, is near enough to caricature to require no further comment; we shall discuss this sort of sociology more fully in chapter 3. You will be able to find many more examples like these in sociological literature and in common usage.

Often the use in this way of a word denoting a collection of people or things stops us from examining the real complexity of the problem. Vulgar marxists are often very guilty of this as well as sociologists. The 'Ruling Class', or the 'Bureaucracy' is held responsible for all social ills, but the actual nature of these groups in specific social situations isn't defined. The approach is very attractive because it enables someone to explain the problems of any society in a simple formula without having to bother to examine the society itself. This kind of 'analysis' once made Marx himself say in exasperation, 'I am not a marxist.'

But it is not only vulgar marxists who make this sort of mistake. In our societies, politicians constantly justify their actions in terms of the 'National Interest' — to have an incomes policy is in the National Interest, to make atomic weapons or to have atomic power stations is in the National Interest, and so on. If we think about it for a moment, the difficulty of defining what really is a 'national interest' is immense. Almost every policy decision affects some groups in a nation more adversely than others. Thus, to say that a decision is in the national interest usually means to identify the interests of one group of the population as the National Interest, while conveniently forgetting the interests of those members of the nation who are not benefited by the decision. By the appeal to nationalism, sectional decisions may appear more palatable to people they *don't* benefit. Finally there is the constant reference to anyone in control, anyone who does things, as 'they'. 'They' are mending the road, 'they' are building a block of flats, and, more importantly, 'they' as opposed to 'us' control decisions in industry, in politics, and in every relationship that people have with officialdom. These latter forms of expression have been considered to be characteristic of the way working class people look at the world (Gouldthorpe and Lockwood, 1963). If the incorrect use of terms such as society, the bureaucracy, and the national interest can serve to con-fuse people as to the real nature of interest groups involved in decisions, so can this dichotomy of 'us' and 'them' indicate that people feel apart, alien from the sources of decisions. It is, or should be, a matter of concern for people in any form of society which is supposed to be democratic. Second, to accept an everyday definition of society as nation state may be misleading because it inhibits us from looking beyond national boundaries for explanations of why people behave and think as they do in a particular country at a particular time.

In this chapter we have not tried to explain directly what sociology is. Rather, we have tried to present a critique and explanation in sociological terms of the one-sided, partial nature of the explanations of sociology that students very often receive. Because we have treated all this in a sociological way, we have been able to introduce some of the jargon commonly found among, and endlessly accumulated by, sociologists. We also dealt with one of the problems which the explanation of behaviour in terms of groups raises; the danger of treating societies, or equivalent terms for conglomerations of people and things, as if they represent real entities. Our idea of what sociology is, what distinguishes it from other disciplines, lies in the way sociologists approach the explanation of phenomena or problems. They seek causes for them in the facts of people's membership of social groups and in the ways in which these groups are related to each other. This is a simple idea, but there are various reasons why it isn't very easy to explain — we have found — to people in our own society. In the next chapter we shall try to sketch some of these reasons.

Chapter two

The individual and society

Resistances to sociological explanation

Many people in this society find it difficult to get hold of the manner of approach to the study of human behaviour that is characteristic of sociology, namely that in terms of group membership, and group organization. Apart from feeling that there isn't anything definite to focus on, students often raise objections based on two main arguments. First, since every individual is different, explanation of individuals in terms of groups is impossible. This argument contains a logical fallacy, as we shall try to demonstrate below. The second argument is that sociological explanation is contrary to the doctrine of free will; with this we have some sympathy, although not in the religious terms in which it is usually expressed. Before considering these arguments, it is worth asking whether there are any features of the socialization of students who take sociology themselves which might lead them towards these views, which are often ideologies, partial self-justifications, rather than rational arguments. We can put the problem this way. What are the pressures which are brought to bear on prospective sociology students before they come to the institution where they learn sociology?

In societies like this one, based on capitalist private property relationships, there is a strong emphasis on individualism, individual competition and achievement and individual responsibility. This is much less marked in other kinds of society, for example, feudal or economically undeveloped societies studied by anthropologists. In various ways this has been noted by the established sociologists of the past. For instance, Max Weber argued that without an individualist ethic, capitalism could not have developed (Weber, 1977; Tawney,

1969). Nowadays, the controllers of large sections of the mass media — both editors, and those who are in a position to exert pressure on them — and of political opinion define success in terms of individual achievement. For the student who will be taking sociology, the way the education system is organized expresses this individualistic ideology in practical ways. For instance, co-operation in schools is usually defined as 'cheating' and discouraged. In school classes individuals are constantly examined for their achievement in different subjects, and ranked against one another. It is also true that there are counter currents to this individualism. They stem from the fact that for the workers in a society based on private property ownership, individualism historically provided no protection. Any improvements in wages and conditions, whether on economic or political levels, have always come from collective action, rather than from isolated individuals, who found themselves powerless. It is not surprising therefore that young people who have been brought up in workers' families have considerable problems of adjustment to the way things are done in the 'upper' levels of the traditional education system, as Jackson and Marsden's study of working class boys in a grammar school has indicated (Jackson and Marsden, 1969). In order to succeed in the education system, students have to learn to compete on this individualistic basis. What sociologists say about the importance of groups seems to challenge their own experience of achievement. The idea is often expressed that people are 'naturally' competitive, or 'naturally' selfish, although it is very easy to show by the use of examples from anthropology that the degree of selfishness or competitiveness that people exhibit depends on the organization of the society from which they come. The frequency with which arguments in defence of individualism are linked with denunciations of communism, or assertions to the effect that a 'classless' society is impossible, indicates that students very often feel that some justification of 'their' society, of 'their' way of life, is involved. In a certain sense, it is.

'All individuals are different', or 'All individuals are unique, *therefore* they can't be explained sociologically.' Let us examine this very common argument against sociological types of explanation. We can look at it in two ways. If it were followed to its logical conclusion it would mean that we could never make any predictions about how anyone would behave. For example, when we go into a café, we are pretty sure that there will be someone to cook the food, and some means of purchasing it. Cooks will cook and food will be sold. If people, in spite of being individuals, did not behave as others expected them to, at least sometimes, the whole of social life would be impossible. The statements that sociologists make are no different in type from the above, except that often broader groups of the population are involved and the links between the groups and the behaviour are less obvious. We expect that people will behave in such a way in a café so that food is provided for us, and we don't need to think about it. We don't necessarily expect that male, protestant divorcees will be more likely to commit suicide than others — as Durkheim showed — and it needs a considerable amount of explanation to indicate why this should be so. The main point is that the *therefore* in the argument above is a logical error. There is no incompatibility between a thing being unique and sharing characteristics with others. Compare two objects: Object A has characteristics p, q, and r. Object B has characteristics p, q, and s. They are alike in that they share characteristics p and q. But they differ from each other in that they do not share characteristics r or s. Human beings have an almost unlimited number of characteristics, and we are able to analyse them sociologically because everyone shares some characteristics with others, as well as having some different ones, which they probably share with someone else. It is the *total* combination which is unique, not every individual characteristic. Thus, logically, human individuality is no barrier to sociological explanation. Since an individual does not respond to a situation in terms of one characteristic alone, but as a whole person, it is clear that the actual prediction of an individual's behaviour in a situation is much more difficult than to make general predictions about the likelihood of particular behaviour occurring in a certain group in specified conditions. The other kind of argument goes, 'The deterministic type of explanations that social scientists use are a denial of free will, and thus degrade people.' This is a more difficult argument because it touches on an old controversy of philosophy — free will versus determinism, and also has direct moral and political overtones. In a narrow sense this argument is mistaken. The fact that there are usually cooks in restaurants does not mean that there is any theoretical impossibility that a given cook might decide not to turn up, and that this might be an exercise of free will. It is true, however, that any social scientist will search for the cause of behaviour in a person's social experience. But, as we have tried to point out in the first chapter, once we are aware of forces pressuring us to behave in certain ways, then a choice as to whether to continue to so behave or not becomes meaningful. If we are not aware of the reasons for our behaviour, we cannot make choices about it. So the study of sociology could extend the choices we can make.

On the other hand, it is justifiable to express irritation at the mechanistic way some sociologists, and some schools of sociology, approach the study of people. Instead of an interaction between people and society — a dialectical relationship — there is a one-way adaptation of people to society, an adaptation buttressed by the use of jargon — such as role, norm and deviant — which we shall discuss further below (Wrong, 1964). Some sociologists have been led towards this one-way approach by the study of undeveloped societies, in which every individual seemed to fit in, and very little behaviour appeared to be unexpected. Everything seemed to be explicable in terms of the groups in the society to which the individual belonged and the way they were related and organized. For other sociologists there lies behind the theories an attempt to justify the 'system', and to explain it in terms that will persuade people who suffer in it not to rise in justified wrath to overthrow it. These arguments are part of our constant attack on that approach to sociology which can be labelled functionalist, and which, in its pervasive varieties and influence, we are seeking to combat throughout this book. Functionalist approaches need criticism, but although to do so by arguing about free will is understandable, it lets the culprit off the hook too easily.

Public issues and personal troubles

So far, we have tried to show that the usual objections to sociological explanations are not well founded, but that the individualistic ideology of this society leads many students to hold rather strongly to these objections. We have also attacked the mechanistic approach to sociology which explains human behaviour in terms of a one-way adaptation of people to society. However, it is vital to recognize the pervasiveness of the social influences, and the importance of sociological explanation in understanding human behaviour and social problems. In our view this involves cultivating a way of looking at social problems, and of trying to explain behaviour, a specific kind of sensitivity. C. Wright Mills, with whose general approach to sociology we are in considerable agreement, has called this the 'sociological imagination', and Gouldner argues for a sociological awareness which he calls reflexive sociology (Mills, 1970; Gouldner, 1971; Shaw, 1975). Mills argues that in the complex modern world of great states and constant change, it is above all this 'imagination' that helps us to ask the right sort of questions so that we can begin to explain the social problems that face us. If one person is unemployed, he says, that is a personal problem for that person, a trouble. As long as there are jobs available, we look to character or training for an explanation. But when a large proportion of a nation's labour force is unemployed, it is impossible to explain this in terms of individuals — we must look to the groups they belong to and their organization, the way society is organized, for an explanation. It becomes an *issue*. Very often wealthy and secure individuals see unemployed people as inadequate or lazy, rather than as the victims of the same social system from which the wealthy benefit. Another example Mills gives is of marriage — if one marriage breaks down, this is a personal problem. When, as in contemporary America, one third of all marriages end in divorce (50 per cent in the Los Angeles area), then, although it appears as a personal problem to each couple, we are justified in seeking an explanation outside the individual couple, in terms of the social significance of marriage and the family and changes in the way women and men relate to one another. Stokely Carmichael makes a similar point in another way, substituting the terms individual and institutionalized for troubles and issues:

> When unidentified white terrorists bomb a black church and kill five black children, that is an act of individual racism, widely deplored by most segments of the world. But when in that same city, Birmingham, Alabama, five hundred black babies die each year because of lack of proper food, shelter and medical facilities, and thousands more are destroyed or maimed physically, emotionally and intellectually because of conditions of poverty and discrimination in the black community, that is a function of institutionalised racism (Carmichael, 1968).

If *troubles* are defined as being largely personal in origin, and *issues* as largely social in origin, Mills argues that, because we experience all events in a personal way, we tend to underestimate the explanation in terms of issues. It is necessary therefore to establish the importance and widespread relevance of the sociological type of explanation. We shall try to do this by considering two areas of study, one of which is often considered to depend largely upon biology, and the other, one of the most personal, individual kinds of problem, in order to show how important it is to be aware of sociological explanations.

Examples of the pervasiveness of social influences

I *Women and men*

Who asks whom to dance? Who usually takes most part in bringing up the children in a marriage? Who does more of the cooking? Who is responsible for the housework? Who is more likely to stop work on marriage? and even more likely to stop on having children? Who is expected to be the breadwinner? Who generally makes sexual advances? Who spends more time on personal adornment? Who is judged by others more in terms of their personal attractiveness than in terms of the work they do or their skills? Hardly anyone will have difficulty in answering these questions, and a majority, though by no means all, will also be describing themselves in giving the answers. What is the reason for the different ways of behaving that most people expect of women and men in our society today? Because there are physiological and biological differences between women and men, it is very often assumed that physiology and biology are directly responsible for these different ways of behaviour. The argument runs that for women and men to behave as they usually do is not a social, but a natural thing. From this it is easy to characterize people who don't behave in expected ways as somehow unnatural. Margaret Mead, in a famous book, *Sex and Temperament in Three Primitive Societies*, set out to show, by using examples from her studies in New Guinea, that many of the differences between the sexes often attributed to biology are, in fact, social in origin (Mead, 1978). One of the advantages of New Guinea as an area of investigation is that, although there are many different societies there, there has been relatively little mixing among them for long periods. Within a relatively small geographical area, many different ways of doing things can be found. The Arapesh tribe, Mead points out, made very little distinction between the ways of behaving of the different sexes. Assertiveness or aggressiveness, which, in our society, are usually attributed to men, are not characteristic of the behaviour of either sex among the Arapesh, among whom there is an uniform lack of ambition. Even the biological fact that women have to have the children is socially minimized. Men lie down with their wives immediately after childbirth, and, by some process of self-suggestion that seems to work for both man and woman, men 'take over' much of the fatigue, lessening the suffering of the woman. We find, however, that in as far as heavy carrying work is done in this primitive society, it is performed by the women, who are supposed to be equipped 'naturally' with specially strong foreheads for the purpose. Mead explains the lack of aggressiveness by reference to the practice of late weaning of children, and the fact that any child will be fed by any mother who can give milk. She compares the Arapesh to the Mundugamor, a tribe of recently 'pacified' head hunters living some distance away. Here aggressiveness was a characteristic of both men and women in equal measure. She describes love-making as a battle between the partners, from which each returns bruised and torn. It is explained that children are reared with extreme disregard, many firstborn being drowned, with adults showing little affection for children. What, however, is clear is that both the characteristics and the childrearing practices of the Arapesh and the Mundugamor are related to the ways they had of procuring their food, which, since they were at subsistence level, was a constant preoccupation. The Arapesh obtained it by cultivating the land; the Mundugamor, to a considerable extent used to kill people from other neighbouring societies. Aggressiveness is not connected with the former, but very relevant to the latter. In a third tribe, the Tchambuli, some of the attributes often ascribed to women and men in our society seemed actually to be reversed. Men adorned themselves, and gos. ped, and were selected by the women, who made sexual advances. Women did all the trade upon which the society depended, although the men made many of the traded items. Women were dominant and aggressive. Mead points to the fact that girls were brought up smoothly within a circle of women, but that boys were thrown out at an early age, and for a period seemed spurned by all, thus becoming insecure and constantly seeking affection. But, it also appears that this society used to be one in which head hunting went on, but that this, for some unspecified reason, became less important, perhaps because of the high value that other groups placed upon the mosquito nets that the Tchambuli learned how to produce. Since the men had been specialized as head hunters, the division of labour in the society had changed, leaving the men with no clear position. It is also interesting to notice that in Tchambuli, the natural and created resources were sufficient to enable attention to be diverted from food gathering so that art could develop.

Here, therefore, we have three societies in which the expectations about how women and men should behave differed widely from those often found in Britain today, and from each other. But how can we tell which behaviour is more natural? No doubt, members of each of the societies would describe their behaviour as natural. By comparing each with the other, and all with our own society, we are driven to the conclusion that the problem is not biological but social. The sources of the behaviour and attitudes of women and men are to be sought in the way in which physiological differences are interpreted in societies arranged in different ways. Margaret Mead compares several societies. She uses the comparative method. This is very helpful for the sort of problem which proposes that certain forms of behaviour are universal, or natural. By investigating the variety of behaviour in different societies we can test whether such statements are true or not. History can be used in the same way, to test the validity of propositions about the universality or naturalness of patterns of behaviour. Perhaps in our own society in previous times, things were done differently, in which case we can explain what we are studying socially.

Another important thing can be noticed about the description of the three societies we have given above. In accounting for the differences in the societies, Mead gives particular emphasis to patterns of bringing up children. The explanation is in terms of socialization. But we have tried to suggest that the method in which a society's wealth (in these cases, food) is produced, and, with the Tchambuli, the change in the basis of production, is also important in regard to both the behaviour, and the form of socialization. From the evidence given, such an explanation seems eminently reasonable. Both things concerned with *production*, the manufacture of things, and *reproduction*, the socialization of people, are important in understanding human behaviour. The different emphasis in explanations illustrates how the things that different sociologists consider important can affect not only their explanantion of *what* they observe, but also what they consider is worth emphasizing in what they observe, bringing us back to the problems of sociologists we talked of in the first chapter.

We have tried to show that something commonly assumed to be biological in origin is, in fact, social, in order to illustrate the pervasiveness of the social, the importance of sociological explanation, which is the main theme of this section. We can also notice that sociological investigation is relevant to the problems about the relationships of women to paid work, homes and childbearing, problems which are frequently considered as 'women's problems' in the media. Particularly since the 1950s, middle class women have more often expected the right to work and there have been more economic pressures for them to do so. Of course, working class women historically have never had the opportunity of such a choice. By and large, where work has been available for them, they have had to take it, out of economic necessity. As working class people have struggled to improve their standards of living, the same kind of choice, and dilemma, begins to become meaningful for some of them.

But a glance at today's world shows us that expectations about women's relationships to family and work are not the same everywhere, but vary from society to society, and are also changing within the same societies. These 'women's problems' derive from the structure of the society, rather than from the women themselves. An interesting United Nations study illustrates this. This study compared psychiatrists' reports of the causes of neurosis in married women with families, in different countries (World Health Organization, 1966). A psychiatrist from Czechoslovakia reported that problems were very frequent among that group of women who were not working, but spent their time at home with their children. Those who combined work with the upbringing of children were less likely to suffer neuroses. On the other hand, a psychiatrist from Spain, reporting on problems of middle class and wealthier Spanish women, reported the opposite. It was those who *did* combine work and child upbringing who had mental strain. How can we reconcile these contradictory reports? The problem is solved once we know that in Czechoslovakia, it is normal for women with young children to do a job, and that in Spain it is not normal for middle class and wealthier women with young children to do a job. It becomes clear that the causes of the problems of the women are social in nature – the problem is that their behaviour is in conflict with the expectations of most of the people with whom they associate, and this gives rise to tensions which are expressed as neuroses. We might also point out that arguments about women's 'biological' specialization as child upbringer, etc., have been utilized to preserve the social, economic and sexual subordination of women (Mitchell, 1971). Whatever type of society we look at, up to now in the vast majority of cases, the powerful positions in its economic, political, military, educational and communications systems have always been overwhelmingly in male hands, its value systems have been dominated by characteristics considered male, and in family and sexual relations violence is frequently used against women to ensure male dominance (Millett, 1971; Brownmiller, 1976; Gersoni-Stavn, 1974; Burris, 1971).

This concentration of overt power in the hands of the male elites is neither inevitable, nor have its results been impressive. On the other hand, women's under-recorded history, now being researched by feminist historians, suggests that the catalogue of exploitation, wars, unfettered egocentrism and distorted ideals – the history of male power – can be supplemented by a distinctly more humane and caring, but still progressive history from the underside of society to which we as women have been relegated in the past (for example, O'Faolain and Martines, 1974; Porter, 1976).

2 Suicide

In our demonstration of the pervasiveness of the social, we have taken an example of relationships widely thought to be biological or 'natural' in origin, and shown that they can only be explained when we know something of the social context in which they occur. Let us take another kind of example to strengthen the point. For most people, the act of *suicide* will seem the most individual of acts, a decision taken by an individual at the utmost extremity of personal despair or depression. And yet it was this problem which was made the subject of one of the most famous of the sociological studies at the turn of the twentieth century, *Suicide*, by Émile Durkheim (1970). One of the reasons why Durkheim himself undertook this study was to try to show that the study of behaviour was not reducible totally to the study of individuals. He wrote in his preface to the book:

> It is not realized that there can be no sociology unless societies exist, and that societies cannot exist if there are only individuals (p. 38).

It was this attack against reducing sociology to psychology that sometimes led Durkheim to overstress his point and give the impression of agelicism which we have discussed in the first chapter. Durkheim made no attempt at all to approach individuals who had attempted suicide, to ask for their reaons. Nor did he seek the co-operation of relatives of known suicides. What he did was to collect together the statistics on the number of suicides for various European countries during the nineteenth century, and to analyse them. A most striking fact emerged. If suicide was an act of individual despair, into which no social components entered, it would be reasonable to expect random variations in suicide rates in any society from year to year. Yet, in spite of the small number of cases compared to the total populations, the suicide *rates* from year to year were remarkably steady, steadier, in fact, than the birth and death rates for particular societies. Durkheim considered carefully all the explanations for suicides that had been put foward up to that time, based on such factors as climate, race, mental

25

illness, heredity, and contagion (the idea that one suicide sparks off another). He demonstrated that all these explanations were untenable, either because they were logically flawed, or because propositons which they entailed could be shown to be untrue when compared with the available statistics. It did become clear, however, that the incidence of suicide was more frequent at some times of the day than others, and at some seasons of the year than others, namely, that it was more frequent in summer than in winter, and more frequent in mid-morning and afternoon than at any other time. Durkheim also found numerous other correlations. We should not think that he discovered them by chance, and then built a theory to account for them, although this is the impression given by the lay out of the book; nor that Durkheim had a ready made theory which enabled him to look for all the 'right' facts. We can assume that his general approach to sociology, in combination with the material of previous research and the results of the researches he carried out, all these, in interaction, led him to the propositions which he finally presented in his book as if they were a logical progression from the particular to the general. It is important to point this out, because the fallacy that theories and models are derived from the accumulation of small pieces of evidence is still quite common in sociology. So is an alternative view that one has to build a whole theory *first*, and then test it afterwards (see chapter 6). Durkheim discovered that the likelihood of suicide was related to the religion that a person belonged to. Protestants were more likely to commit suicide than Catholics, and Jews were least prone of all. Suicide was also related to the type of family life people led. Married people with children were less likely to commit suicide than unmarried people or widows and widowers. For women who were, or had been married, those who did not have children committed suicide more frequently. He also noticed that suicide rates were reduced at times when important political events which involved people were occurring, such as crucial elections, popular wars, etc., Durkheim was able to see a common link in all these relationships. It was the degree of integration of the individual into the society. Protestant religious beliefs, with their emphasis on the direct relationship between an individual and God (or their conscience), do not provide such a complete framework of integration as the Catholic, while Jewish religious beliefs and institutions are the most integrative of all. The unmarried, widowed, are not as well integrated into a family unit, while the fact that suicide is reduced where there is greater political activity of a popular nature suggests that political integration is also related to suicide. Durkheim put forward three propositions. The likelihood of suicide will vary, he said, inversely with the degree of religious, family and political integration. The more an individual is integrated into one or all of these spheres, the less the likelihood of suicide. From this he proposed a type of suicide which he calls egoistic, caused by lack of social integration. The explanation of why suicide occurs more frequently in the summer and in late morning and afternoon also follows logically from this proposition, because it is at these seasons and times that there is most interaction among people in European societies, so a person who is not integrated feels it most at these times.

Durkheim also noticed two other, general features. First, suicide was much more common in towns, and secondly, suicide rates had tended to increase over the century. Durkheim argued that life in towns was more impersonal, 'anomic', than life in the country, and that the process of industrialization in the nineteenth century was increasing the importance of the towns. It appeared that to some extent, the framework for integration was itself breaking down, so that it was becoming less easy for individuals to be integrated. Durkheim was very concerned with this trend, which he considered indicated a degree of social illness, social pathology, and he suggested that there was a second type of suicide, anomic, deriving from situations where the individual had no stable framework into which to integrate.

Finally, Durkheim noticed that people also killed themselves in situations where there was a very high degree of integration of the individual into the social group, as in primitive or traditional societies, and in the officer corps in the armed services. He concluded from this that, in some social situations people could be so highly integrated into society that they value their own lives less than the acceptance of the social demands made on them. Either for honour, or for shame at some transgression of these social demands, they would sacrifice their lives to maintain or reinforce either the cause or the social system with which they so strongly identified. This led Durkheim to posit a third category of suicide, which he named altruistic.

Subsequent research has modified but not invalidated Durkheim's statistical findings, but the particular detail of this or that proposition is not what concerns us here (Giddens, 1965; 1966). What Durkheim succeeded in demonstrating is that the individual act of suicide, isolated and infrequent though it is, cannot be explained without the consideration of the social relationships which all individuals in various ways depend upon. It should be noted that this kind of approach does not enable us to predict which individual will commit suicide, but only to predict those social groups from which suicides will most frequently come, and why. It is also not possible to accept Durkheim's proposition that there was a sort of social pathology involved in increasing suicide rates. Different social groups, in different positions in social structures, have different ideas as to what is socially desirable or undesirable. So do the same groups in different historical circumstances. For these reasons an agreed social pathology is unlikely — aspects of this argument will be developed further in the next chapter. We have used Durkheim's work to illustrate one simple, but very important, indeed crucial argument: the pervasiveness of the social. The two examples we have chosen from very diverse fields are meant to drive this point home.

Roles

At the beginning of the chapter, when attacking the argument against sociology in terms of free will, we indicated our dissatisfaction with the sort of sociology that relates societies and people in terms of the adjustment of people to society. These approaches to sociology all derive from functionalism, which will be criticized later. If there is any one idea which illustrates the grosser crudities of the 'one-way adjustment' approach, it is that of *role*, and, since a lot of sociology students are sure to be told that the idea of role is the key to the understanding of the relationship between society and person, it is certainly worth while giving some consideration to it here, so as not to let such sociologists have it all their own way.

One general difficulty is the vague way in which the term is so often used in sociological work. The first thing, when you find 'role' being extensively used, is to notice how it is defined by the particular writer, or whether, as is often the case, readers are left to attach to the term whatever meaning they wish. One can ask: does role denote a social position — shop steward, surgeon, student? Does it describe how people in such a position actually behave, 'perform their part'? Does it describe how other people expect a surgeon or shop steward to behave? If the latter, which people's expectations prescribe the role? In the case of a shop steward, will it be the expectations of management, fellow workers, or trade union officials? Why one rather than another? Does role refer to a position in a particular situation — the surgeon in the operating theatre — or does the 'role' follow the holder of the position around? Does society have 'needs' which people fulfil by playing roles? Arising out of all this, what view of people and society is implicit in role theory? The term role comes from acting, of course. Actors playing roles in the theatre are performing for others parts whose outline has been drawn, not by themselves, but by the author of the play. The actors are deliberately not themselves, but performers. Because society, the social, is so pervasive, as we have tried to show, sociologists have often been tempted to argue that all of us are in fact playing parts, not laid down by an author, but by 'society' — an idea we have already criticized. The appeal of this analogy may partly lie in the fact that sociologists are members of groups (middle class, upwardly mobile, academic) among whom the playing of parts, more or less deliberately, forms a considerable amount of social life, and the success with which one plays these parts, the impressions one creates, are ways of gaining status and recognition from one's fellows (cf. the popularity of Goffman's theory about the management of appearances amongst up and coming sociologists in the late 1960s (Goffman, 1971)).

The idea seems to get a boost from sociologists' own social experience. Moreover role appears to have become an indispensable concept for much of the sociology which services professional training courses, and this has been a growth area for the employment of sociologists from the mid 1960s until quite recently. Courses for teacher and social work training, for example, are generally designed to socialize new recruits to see themselves as 'professionals', identifying their interests with those of their employers — the school, the agency, etc. A sociology which talks to teaching and social work students about 'the role of the teacher', 'the role of the social worker' thus provides both description and justification (but no explanation) of the pressures against criticism and imagination which are so often a part of the process of professional socialization.

So many sociologists have been encouraged to go on developing the idea of social life as role playing; everyone seems to be acting all the time. For example: Professor Banton, in his book, *Roles* (1965), which is, in effect, an introduction to sociology, argues that almost all human behaviour and almost all the ideas of sociology can be interpreted in terms of 'role theory'.

The fundamental difficulty with such a view is that it assumes that there is, or ought to be, agreement about how people in particular positions should behave:

For the time being it is necessary to assume in the examination of particular roles that there is agreement among all the parties affected as to the definition of the role in question (Banton, 1965, p. 36).

29

> People expect appropriate behaviour from the holder of a particular
> position. The sum of these expectations is the role (Frankenberg,
> 1970, pp. 16–17).

There is no reason why we should not replace the word 'role' with the
word 'stereotype' in these examples – to do so reveals the determinism
of the argument. The reader is referred also to the example from
Berger (1970) discussed on p. 13. It is important to ask whether it is
valid to start with such assumptions, and whether we can add together
the expectations of different people and thus find what a particular
role is. Let us do so by taking an example – the social position of the
schoolteacher.

Teachers exist in many societies, and have existed over many centuries; within this country at the present time they may be employed
by local authorities or by private bodies; they may be women or
men; their pupils may be five to fifty years old, and come from any
social background; they may teach in a large city or a remote rural
area. Before we talk about the 'teacher's role' in general we should
have to establish that there were common elements everywhere and
at all times which go beyond the general definition of teacher. However, even if we decide on the exact structural location of the teacher
in a particular type of school, we must also take into account all the
different groups of people who have some interest in what she does.
These would include the other teachers in the school, the pupils, the
headteacher, the parents, the HMIs, the local authority advisers, and
administrators, education college tutors, and so on. How do these
people think that teacher should behave? How far can we assume that
they will agree? Studies by Gross (1967) in the USA, and by Musgrove
and Taylor (1969) in Britain, indicate that, while such different groups
may have particular expectations of school superintendents or school
teachers, there may not be agreement between the groups as to what
is expected. In an attempt to avoid the undercutting of the whole
concept of role which these disagreements imply, the idea of role conflict is generally introduced to describe situations where there are
conflicting expectations of the holder of a particular position. Merton
(1964) has played down the significance of these conflicts, because
some of the groups of people involved are not very powerful, or do
not actually see what the teacher does. Power relationships are not
static, however, and the expectations of those who cannot directly
observe the teacher may none the less be important.

Although these, and endless other elaborations of 'role theory' have to acknowledge the existence of conflicting expectations, the assumption that consensus somehow ought to exist is not discarded; if it were, the whole basis of role theory would collapse. We can see that people's notions of how those in particular social positions (teacher, waitress, students etc.) should behave vary according to their own group membership. We have already discussed the way in which individuals may be influenced by the expectations which others have of them. Role theory can be seen as an attempt to deal with the processes of stereotyping which go on in society. But because it makes the stereotype the role, it blocks us off from an understanding of the contradictory expectations which affect people in many social situations. It is the development of such contradictory expectations which creates some possibility of challenging even dominant ideas about how people should behave.

If, instead of talking about roles, we talk about the expectations held by specified groups as to the behaviour of people in certain positions, it makes it much easier to check the consequences of these expectations. It leads us away from the sort of mechanical idea of sociology that society 'creates', via social organization, sets of roles to which a person 'has to' conform, an idea which underlies the thinking of many sociologists. Definition in terms of expectations gives a much more flexible, dynamic model, in which people's behaviour in positions depends on an interaction between their own learned expectations and the pressures put upon them by others with possibly different expectations. It also depends on the power others have over them, an interaction which will be in constant conflicting change as power relationships change — in other words, a dialectical relationship. Reverting to the example of the school teacher, the approach used by Webb in his article, 'The Sociology of a School' (1962), in which he examines the varying types of pressures which will face a teacher in a slum secondary modern school, offers a potentially more adaptable and dynamic perspective than can be found in most writing on the 'teacher's role' in the sociology of education texts. (See also Hammersley and Woods, 1976.)

In general, the theorizing about roles appears to us to be one of the most arid areas of sociological endeavour. It has started from inadequate ideas and built up mountains of qualifications and sub-qualifications. Role theory is an occupation which can keep a pedantic brain busy for years and even secure career advancement, but it tells us virtually nothing at all about the world we live in (e.g. Biddle and Thomas, 1966). The danger of actually confusing an analogy with

31

whatever it is supposed to illuminate (a danger which we shall examine further in the next chapter) can be illustrated here, too. When Goffman views social life as a play, with people as role-takers, actors, performers (only one of the analogies he develops), he tends to slip into the sort of mistakes we have called agelicism, even though his more acute observations of human behaviour are of the adaptations which people make to social situations which they do not control, whether patients in mental hospitals, surgeons in the operating theatres or islanders in the Shetlands (Goffman, 1969; 1970; 1971). Although Goffman is interested in social interactions, he remains locked in a deterministic theory of the relations between society and people. Role theory in general has been criticized in greater detail by Coulson, 1972.

Chapter three

Social structure

Understanding social structure

Apart from the development of the idea of the pervasiveness of the social, our approach up to now has tended to be negative – a series of warnings against uncritical acceptance of what is taught as sociology. As we criticized, we introduced some sociological ideas and methods of analysing problems. The approaches we have criticized are still common in the USA and in Britain. This is especially true in school sociology syllabuses, for 'O' and 'A' level exams. What positive alternative are we giving?

A considerable number of sociologists pay lip service to the idea of social structure. In our view, providing it is linked with the ideas of social conflict and social change, the idea of social structure is a key leadoff point, and the anchorage idea of sociology. It isn't, however, a completely easy idea to grasp operationally, that is, in use, nor is there agreement among sociologists as to how it should be used or indeed whether it is the central idea at all. In developing your own views on the subject it will be necessary to compare our arguments with those of others.

The idea of social structure is as difficult to define in a few words as is sociology itself (but see Bottomore, 1977, ch. 7). We think of it as a guide which tells us where to look in trying to explain any social phenomenon sociologically. The explanation of the social phenomenon, or part, or individual in a society should be sought first in the way that society is organized as a whole, in its principles of organization. If you like, social structure is a signpost to the right questions to ask.

All this is very abstract; in order to clarify it, and to develop the idea, we are going to use a simple analogy, and later give some examples from anthropological studies. One analogy, which a large number of sociologists have used in the past in order to try to indicate the way they think that social phenomena ought to be explained, is called the 'organic analogy', and it compares societies to organisms (Radcliffe-Brown, 1963, ch. 9; Durkheim, 1964). We do not like this analogy, because it is easy to become so involved in it that one begins to forget that it is an analogy at all, and to come to believe that societies really *are* like organisms. We use instead the analogy of a watch, both positively, to suggest why structure is important, and negatively, to show how plausible are some of the mistakes noted sociologists have made.

The watch analogy

The most important point to start with is: a watch is more than the sum of its parts. If you have a watch handy as you read this, take it to pieces. Collect all the parts together and put them in your hand. You do not have a watch, but a heap of parts. Therefore, a watch is not just the sum of its parts, but the sum of its parts *plus* the way they are put together, related to each other, organized. In the same way, society is more than the sum of the people in it. It is not only the people, but also the way they are related to each other, organized — the social structure. What goes on in society can't be explained solely in terms of individuals, but only by understanding the ways they are placed in relation to each other.

The analogy may be developed. A watch can be subdivided into groups of parts — for instance, those connected with the power supply; with regulation; with information; with protection. Within larger groups of parts are smaller groups, till one gets back to the individual part. Some sociologists, using the organic analogy, have tried to say that societies have regulative systems, digestive systems, etc., in the same way as a body has. This use of the analogy is completely misleading. We are *not* trying to say that any particular group of parts in a watch, those connected with information, say (hands, dial, etc.), has an equivalent in society. We are arguing that, as the action of each part is explained by the organization of its group of parts, and the action of its group by the organization of the whole, the structure, so, in society, we can partly explain the action of individuals by the organization of the groups to which they belong, and the action of the groups partly by the organization of the whole society, the social structure. Notice the modifications to the analogy here. First, to claim a total explanation in terms of structure would be an extreme example of the crude determinism which we have attacked earlier, as well as expecting too much of sociology and denying other social sciences, especially psychology, the right to part of the explanation. Second, the same individual, unlike a watch part, belongs to various different groups, so things are not so neat as in a watch. But if we think simply of the relation between the parts of a watch and the whole, and suggest that it can be subdivided in terms of subsidiary groups of parts, so we can think of the relation between an individual and social structure, and subdivide it in terms of subsidiary concepts, such as those of institutions and groups. A very simplified little diagram shows what we mean.

Initial stage in explaining individual behaviour sociologically:

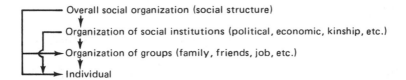

Overall social organization (social structure)

Organization of social institutions (political, economic, kinship, etc.)

Organization of groups (family, friends, job, etc.)

Individual

Explore the relationships suggested by the arrows, but please note that the diagram is at this stage static and one-way. It requires considerable modification.

Let's play with the analogy with a watch a little further. The parts and groups of parts in a watch have a closely defined action in the structure of a watch. The watch is designed for a specific purpose – to tell the time. There can be very little variation in the action of the parts of our watch, since, if they don't do exactly what they are made to do, they are faulty, and we say that the watch is wrong. Perhaps the part is faulty – badly made. Alternatively, the design of the watch may be faulty, so that it puts excessive strain on one group of parts. At this point we think the watch analogy becomes very misleading.

Unlike a watch, there is no external creator of society, nor is there any externally defined purpose for it. Societies are created by the parts (people) of the structure themselves interacting. Since there is no external creator, and no external purpose, it is quite possible that the views of groups of people within the structure may conflict with regard to what purposes the society has, or should have. But we cannot say that there is something wrong either with the people or with the 'design'. Although it is theoretically as possible to design societies as it is watches, and several people have put forward blueprints as to how they think society ought to be designed (Auguste Comte, who gave sociology its name, was a dab hand at this — see Mill, 1961), generally speaking, no one designed the societies that people have lived in up to now. Like Topsy, they just growed. We have to find out how, and why.

Unlike watch parts, therefore, designed for a purpose, persons, groups and institutions may not 'fit in'. Unlike in a watch, conflicts of interest between persons and groups may be part of a social structure in a way they never could be in a watch. Indeed, as we shall show in the next chapter, one of the main ways of understanding how societies change is by examining the conflicts of interests between different groups, who are in different positions in a social structure, and the different benefits they receive from being in these positions.

Varieties of functionalism

We have argued that societies, unlike watches, have no external purpose. But a large number of sociologists disagree with this. They attempt to explain society *teleologically* (by attributing a purpose to it). Particularly those sociologists studying primitive societies observed that in many cases, things there really did seem to be a little analogous to a watch — people and groups seemed to fit together rather like the parts of a watch. In order to make sense of what they saw, they developed the following sorts of explanation, which also underlie the way many sociologists today look at societies. Some argued that the purpose of society was the maintenance of social order, and social stability, and that the function of the parts of a society and the way they were organized, the social structure, was to maintain this order and stability. Radcliffe-Brown, a famous British anthropologist, expounded this view (Radcliffe-Brown, 1963). It is still very influential, and we can call it *structural functionalism*. Another argument was that the purpose of society is the satisfaction of certain biological needs of human beings (Malinowski, 1944, pp. 145f.). This can be characterized as *biological functionalism*, and it is not so popular, or so widely used in contemporary sociology as the former (Gluckman, 1944). A third view is a more sophisticated development of the first. It is based on the idea that the maintenance of order, or equilibrium (another analogy, borrowed from mechanics), is largely achieved by the existence of common values, or norms, shared by the vast majority of the people in the society. The emphasis on norms, rather than on structure, leads this view, popular in the USA and among a number of sociologists in Britain, to be called *normative functionalism*. Its central theorist is Talcott Parsons (Parsons, 1970; Black, 1976; Giddens, 1968; Lessnoff, 1968; Foss, 1963 — the last four references are critiques). If the central purpose, the maintenance of order, is accepted, then it is possible to carry the watch analogy further, for instance, to suggest that some parts of a society may be ill, or pathological (which sounds better), because they don't fit in. Durkheim's contention that the suicide rate increase in nineteenth-century Europe represented pathological development in the societies in the period is an example of this idea. Elton Mayo, a well-known American management sociologist, argued that shop stewards in industry who were seen as non-cooperative by management were in some way ill (Mayo, 1975). The basic fault with all these views is that it is a complete mistake to attribute any sort of purpose at all to society, which, as we have argued above, is not a *thing* like a watch at all, but a collective term for a defined group of people, their possessions, organization and behaviour and the inter-relationship of all these.

Only people can have purposes. Groups of people in common situations may have common purposes. What these may be, and how they are related to the organization of the society is a matter for investigation. It cannot be decided in advance on theoretical grounds. In spite of this basic mistake, functionalism has been very popular, for two main reasons. First, it seems to provide a way of giving order to the tremendous complexity of the whole that makes up a society. It tries to by-pass what people *say* are the reasons for their actions, by establishing an alternative basis of explanation for them — we shall see the advantages of this in the examples which follow. Second, it is very attractive to those groups in a social structure who benefit from maintaining things as they are, since it provides a sophisticated ideology to justify the status quo. Because of this there has always been a conservative element in functionalist sociology (cf. Nisbet, 1970). In case you think that this kind of view is just confined to sociology, it should be pointed out that the same approach underlies the statements of people who say, for instance, that hippies are indicators of social decline, or that strikers are 'harming the national interest'. Unlike in a watch, harmony among the parts of society is *not* an essential part of the structure, so that it is almost impossible to get total agreement as to what the 'national interest' is. As we showed in the first chapter, what one group of people consider to be in the 'national interest' may not be accepted as such by another group.

Sociologists who reject functionalism in all its forms as a means of understanding society, argue that because society is *not* actually like a watch, or a body, it is necessary to analyse the interests and purposes of groups of people in a society, and see how they interrelate. In other words, we need to study social structure without attributing to a society, the characteristics of a person. Because almost all such studies show that actual social structures have developed in such a way that the structure benefits some groups at the expense of others, a potential conflict exists between groups in the social structure, built into the structure itself. Sociologists who adopt this method of analysis of societies, which derives from Marx, are often called *structural conflict* theorists, or advocates of *historical* or *dynamic structuralism* (Lefebvre, 1968).

The watch analogy has enabled us to make several points. It shows the importance of structure as a means of explanation in sociology. It explains the part in terms of the organization of the whole. It differentiates between those sociologists who attribute some purpose to society, providing a *function* for the parts, and those sociologists who do not. This basic difference in approach leads to several other differences in emphasis. One of these has already been introduced in the discussion of role, and others will be discussed later. A further important point, must be introduced here. If our reference point for analysis of societies is some existing purpose, which is always there, the history of how things came to be that way is separate from the explanation of them. It ceases to be of central interest. To talk about the social structure is to describe how the organization of society 'maintains' order. On the other hand, if societies themselves do not have a purpose, the only way we can understand the relationships of groups is by examining how they interact over time — in their historical practice. By examining this — how some groups benefit and others react, for instance — we can find out the principles by which the society is organized, its social structure, and from this, the pressures for change and the resistances to it. In functionalist sociology, therefore, the study of history and change is at a discount — as can be seen from the contents' list of Broom and Selznick's book given in the first chapter. In structural conflict sociology, it is essential — see the contents list of Fiamengo's book. Discussion of this point is continued in chapters 4 and 6.

Culture

A large number of American sociologists assign the concept of structure a subordinate place to that of culture (e.g. Benedict, 1961; Linton, 1961). The argument may be expressed in its simplest form like this. Most sociologists are now agreed that instinct is of little significance in explaining human behaviour, which overwhelmingly derives from what we learn. What we learn derives from our culture − the sets of established ways of doing things developed in a society. Individuals, as they grow up, are *socialized* (trained) or *internalize* (accept as their own) this culture. Therefore, the central concept in explaining behaviour is culture:

Culture → Social Learning → Individual

Most of these sociologists are heavily influenced by Freudian psychology, arguing that the really important learning period is in early childhood. Returning to our analogy for a moment, humans are, in this view, a bit like watch parts − once they are made (in early childhood), they don't change. Once again, these views seem plausible when we study some primitive societies − examples have been given of Margaret Mead's studies of sex and temperament, where she explains different behaviour and attitudes in men and women in terms of different child upbringing in different societies. But this approach gives no explanation − other than historical accident − of why cultures differ, both between societies, and − most importantly when studying our own societies − among different groups of people within societies (Worsley, 1957). The key to this problem lies in understanding how the way a society is organized has developed. It places structure before culture:

Social Structure → Culture → Social Learning → Individual.

This is why, in our use of Mead's work in the second chapter, we have added to her explanations. Furthermore, while acknowledging the importance of the early years of life in explaining behaviour, we would want to emphasize that, in any complex society, many differing and often potentially conflicting ideas are learned by the young. We also need an approach which acknowledges the importance of later socialization in explaining behaviour (cf. Orlansky, 1949; Lindesmith and Strauss, 1950).

Analytic and descriptive uses

We have attempted to introduce the idea of structure analytically, i.e., as a means of understanding the principles behind the inter-relationship of social groups in a society, and of how these inter-relationships developed and are developing. This is the usage adopted by Marx and by Lévi-Strauss, the famous French anthropologist (Godelier, 1967). There is another way of using the idea of structure, so that it is much more *descriptive*, a sort of catalogue of the institutions of a society. This is the approach adopted by Nadel, who distinguishes it clearly from Lévi-Strauss's:

> For Lévi-Strauss and Leach, structure is an explanatory construct meant to provide the key to the observed facts of social existence ... I consider social structure, ... to be still the social reality itself, or an aspect of it, not the logic behind it; and I consider structural analysis to be no more than a descriptive method, however sophisticated, not a piece of explanation (Nadel, 1969).

There is obviously no harm in describing the institutions of a society, but unless one has some explanatory principles, it is impossible to know what to single out as worthy of description. This is why such descriptive uses generally smuggle in *implicit* explanatory principles. The same distinction is often made when we use the term structure in everyday language. For instance, if we say that a building is a structure, this directs our attention to a description of its features, the number and position of its windows, its type of roofing, its shape, etc. If we say that it has a structure, this directs our attention to the means that the designer has adopted to ensure that it doesn't collapse. (But remember that no one designs societies, and that social structure does not exist to ensure that they don't collapse.) Of course, just as analysis involves description, so the analytic use of the idea of structure in sociology involves the descriptive use, but the former is more important, since it gives us a means of explaining things.

Structure and behaviour

It may help in understanding things sociologically if we give a very simple analytic schema of the way structure can affect behaviour, remembering the simple diagram we have introduced above, and that the relationships are not simply one way. The way a society is organized might be thought of as affecting an individual's behaviour directly, by compelling people to do something, or by stopping them from doing something. It might affect their behaviour indirectly, so that, while it is not impossible for them to choose different behaviour, they are more or less strongly pressured, either towards or away from behaving in a particular way. An example illustrates each condition. In a primitive society with a very restricted division of labour, there is only one path that a person can take in life. In Arapesh society, people till the tribe's gardens. In that very simple society, in which the structure lies in the people's mode of production, there is a direct positive influence on a person's behaviour. In our society, action is directly limited by the structure in many respects. For instance, in the area of job choice, investigators have noted that more people wish to get printing apprenticeships than there are jobs available (Pallister, 1938; Veness, 1962). Some *must* therefore be disappointed.

More generally, in a society like ours, where the prestige of occupations, is pyramidal in type — i.e., the better a job, the fewer there are of them — the idea that anybody with sufficient talent can get to the top, though commonly expressed in this country and even more in the USA, is an absolute impossibility. However capable the general population is, only a tiny proportion can fill the small number of jobs at the top.

In our complex societies, very diverse patterns of behaviour are theoretically open to every individual. Therefore, the understanding of indirect pressures, working via socialization and culture, varying according to a person's position in the social structure, becomes very important for the explanation of why individuals behave in one way rather than another. We have already discussed this kind of influence in the first chapter, in relation to sociologists themselves. Here is another simple example. How many young people in our society have read the Communist Manifesto? An enquiry in the basic sociology class of a Scottish university over three years gave a proportion of rather under 3 per cent for that social group. However, almost 100 per cent have read the Bible (at least, parts of it). Without having done any investigation, it is reasonable to suppose that the figures would be reversed in the Soviet Union. Now, it is not prohibited to read the Bible in the Soviet Union, nor the Communist Manifesto in this country. The differences are not the result of chance. It is not adequate to say that they just reflect the differing cultures in the two countries, because, in fact, this is only saying that it is due to chance in a more sophisticated way. Although it comes nearer to an explanation, it is not adequate to say that these books serve in some way to maintain the social order, social stability or equilibrium in the different societies. Their argument assumes that societies have some such order-maintaining purposes built in — the functionalist line of argument which we have already attacked. In order to understand the different importance of the two books in the different societies, we have to analyse the means dominant groups in the societies, in their historical struggle to achieve and maintain their dominance, have used to try to *legitimize* the social structure that results. This is a complex problem in the sociology of social consciousness, the general subject of chapter 5. This approach does not necessarily mean that some smaller or larger group of people sat down and decided this or that. Sometimes groups of people do make such decisions, affecting social events and behaviour. Very often though things develop as by-products of decisions or lack of them in other areas of social life, or, most importantly, as a result of interactions between groups in a social structure.

International structures and interactions between structures

We have so far examined the idea of social structure with respect to individual societies. No society remains totally without contact with other societies. To some extent, therefore, its social structure is affected by others. In some primitive societies, this contact does not seem of great importance. But in others the whole social organization is based on it (Malinowski, 1961). Throughout human history, great empires have been a feature of civilization, so that, for instance, to examine the structure of Jewish society at the time of Christ, without examining its relations with the Roman empire and *its* organization would clearly lead to a very incomplete and faulty understanding.

Today, we are ceaselessly being told about how small the world is becoming, how nations are interdependent, etc., yet a very small proportion of sociologists consider international structural relations in examining social phenomena. Not only do we have to put up with a historyless sociology, but with an insular sociology as well. One of the most glaring examples of this is in the study of the poor countries of the world — the so-called 'Third World' — where sociologists from the 'developed' countries usually totally ignore the historical development of structural relations between the poor and the rich nations (for exceptions to this see Barratt-Brown, 1970; Frank, 1973; and Jalee, 1970 among others). The varieties of possible relationships between nations are large, and their effects on different groups within national social structures may be very different (see Frank, 1967 for examples). This means that the equation between society and nation state may be an unsatisfactory one, because it will be impossible to analyse the social structure of any nation state fully without some reference to its relationships with other nation states. Although countless courses have been taught on the social structure of modern Britain, which look at class, religion, education, family, etc. in Britain, such an approach is not really justifiable. For example, it is not possible to understand class relations, life styles and living standards within Britain without reference to contemporary and historical relations which Britain has and has had with other countries. Similarly, although many studies of race relations and immigration in Britain pay little or no attention to Britain's history as a colonial power, it is impossible to understand patterns of immigration or patterns of prejudice without reference to the colonial past. We cannot go further here than to say that any sociology which does not give international relationships adequate weight is a pseudo-science, a statement which becomes more self-evidently true with every day that passes, for never have interactions between nations developed at such a pace (Riddell, 1972; Mandel, 1975, chs 2, 10, 11).

Examples from social anthropology

We introduced the idea of social structure with the help of an analogy; perhaps some examples will help to clarify the method of structural analysis, and differentiate it from the functionalist approach. When Gluckman studied the Zulu people of South East Africa, he found that each year there was a ceremony to celebrate the goddess Nomkubulwana, who was the goddess of crop fertility (Gluckman, 1955). During this ceremony, the women took over the jobs, the behaviour and even the clothes of the men, who remained in the huts, and were liable to be attacked if they went near the women. What is the explanation for this reversal of normally expected behaviour? If we were to ask a member of the society, we should be told that, by pleasing the goddess, it ensured good harvest. Since to us there would appear to be no good reason why the practice should actually lead to greater fertility, we are led to reject this explanation and to seek another. Following Merton, we could call this explanation, given by the members of the society themselves, the *manifest* one (Merton, 1964, ch. 1). We are searching for another kind of explanation, however, which may not

43

be recognized by the people themselves — this is the *latent* explanation. (Since Merton is a functionalist, he talks of the manifest and latent functions of actions. We prefer to think of the manifest and latent explanations of actions.) An ordinary traveller observing the ritual sees it simply as bizarre, perhaps evidence of the 'backwardness of the natives'; a cultural anthropologist sees it as evidence of the rich diversity of human behaviour. A structural functionalist gets much further. The constant question is, 'How does what goes on function to maintain the social order'? This question gives a way into the problem. On further study, it becomes clear that in several ways the women have a pretty hard time of it in Zulu society. The practice can then be seen to be a ritual 'let out' for the frustrations of the women, a kind of safety valve, so that for one day they can take over, the psychological release obtained making the other 364 days bearable. In this way, the functionalist argues, social order is maintained, and the ritual has a function. We may interpret this example in an alternative way, avoiding the metaphysics involved in attributing to society the purpose of maintaining order, by asking the question, 'In whose interests is the society organized; which social group benefits at the expense of others?' By analysing social practice in the society over time, it becomes clear that the men benefit at the expense of the women. We are led to the conclusion that the ritual has developed as a way by which the subordination of the women to the men in the society is reinforced. It is a safety valve, a yearly ritual, by means of which tensions arising from the constant potential conflict created by the *patriarchal* structure — the dominance of the men over the women — are deflected. It reduces the likelihood of attempts by the women to change the structure to their own advantage. Rituals of a similar character to this (in which a dominant group becomes subordinate for a day, and a subordinate group dominant) are not infrequent. Roman officers served their men once a year, and it is often reputed that in British public schools fags were served by their superiors on one day. Ritual is one way in which subordinate groups can be induced to accept their subordination. The annual ceremony becomes worth while for the dominant groups, analogous to an insurance premium. Once again, there is no suggestion that a group of Zulu men sat down and decided that the women were getting troublesome, so it was necessary to devise a new ritual to keep them quiet. The ritual developed as the structure did, and people in the society more or less genuinely believe that it is a fertility ritual. Only an analysis of the structure gives us a means of 'demystifying' the practice.

Here is another, more detailed example, taken from Oberg's study of the Uganda Ankole (Oberg, 1961), first published in 1940. It referred to the structure of the society before the British colonial period. We ought to note straight away that the study is an historical reconstruction, and that the organization and practices described no longer exist. Oberg attempts to add a time dimension to his study, in spite of the fact there there is no written history, by making cautious use of legends and fireside stories told by the Ankole people. Ankole society has certain resemblances to the feudal society of medieval Europe, which could equally have been used as an example to illustrate ideas of structure put forward here.

The Ankole live in an area between Lake Victoria and the Ruwenzori mountain mass, an area which is reasonably fertile, capable of providing resources surplus to the minimum needs of the population, even with very simple agricultural methods. Historically, if the legends are to be believed, the Bairu (serfs), peasant agriculturalists, were invaded by a group of pastoralists displaced from the north by wars, a group smaller in numbers, but superior in fighting ability. They were able to conquer the Bairu and to settle in the country. This group was called the Bahima (nobles). The stories also tell of another invasion by a still more militarily capable group, who moved on but left one of their number behind to be king over the land. From him all later kings are descended. Whatever the details, it appears that the Bahima conquered the Bairu, and, over time, a social structure developed in which the dominance of the former was established. Ankole was surrounded by other societies of similar social organization and there were frequent wars or raids between them. A remarkable succession ritual existed in Ankole.

When a king seemed to be becoming infirm, he was given poison by court magicians, and a new king selected in the following way. A powerful Muhima (kingmaker, singular form of Bahima) took the sacred drum (the church) — the symbol of supreme religious and secular authority, the perfect king — and hid it. Then all the king's sons — there were usually many, as the king had the right to any virgin in the kingdom as his wife — with the exception of the favourite son, took what followers they could from the court, and fought battles till all but one had been killed or driven into exile. Only the powerful Bahima in the border regions did not take part in these battles. Then the winner fought it out with the favourite son and his followers, the eventual winner of this fight being awarded the drum and the kingship by the kingmaker. The whole process might take six or eight months. During this time, there was a state of partial chaos in the kingdom, with people

45

taking the opportunity of settling old scores by blood revenge. Meanwhile, at the court, the Bairu servants elected a mock 'king' who 'reigned' over the court Bairu until the struggle for the real kingship was over. He was then ceremonially beheaded by the incoming king. Without a theory of social structure, all this appears as bizarre – a grotesque example of primitivism. It was reported as such by early travellers from Europe visiting the region, such as Burton and Speke. Functionalists can do much better. By reference to the universal principle of the maintenance of order which societies 'have', they can show that the practices of the Ankole succession help to keep the existing order going. Although this is much better than nothing, as we have shown, it is based on a false premise – the reification of society into a being that can have purposes. In our view, the key to the explanation of the Ankole practices involves an understanding of the social structure. The key to this is given by the area's history, which, sketchy though it is, indicates that the social structure favours the Bahima as a social group, in terms of wealth and power. Oberg analysed the relations between the Bahima and the Bairu in detail. The Bairu had to give tribute to the Bahima in grain and labour. They were not allowed to own productive cows, the Bahima's 'status symbol'. No Mwiru (singular form of Bairu) could marry a Muhima, nor could Bairu become Bahima in any other way – their positions were *ascribed* (fixed by birth). Bahima could take blood revenge against Bairu who they considered to have wronged them, but Bairu had no right of blood revenge against Bahima. Furthermore, although there were frequent wars, all the fighting was done by the Bahima, because no Mwiru was allowed to possess weapons. Thus the Bairu as a group were in every way subordinate to the Bahima. A potential conflict between the groups is built into the structure. From the striving by the Bahima, the dominant group, to stop the potential conflict from becoming real, explanations for the events emerge. Thus, although the military potential of the Ankole was weakened by the refusal to allow the Bairu to have arms, it was necessary for the Bahima, in case the more numerous Bairu turned weapons against the Bahima. Now we can begin to understand the part of the succession ritual concerning the mock Mwiru 'king'. In this ritual, the potential aspirations of the Bairu to a different social position are recognized. The beheading of the 'king' is a dramatization of the consequences of such an attempt. This is another way in which the Bairu were kept from trying to change their positions, derived from the symbolic aspects of the kingship and the Sacred Drum (served by priests). These were supposed to provide justice, so that

Bairu could appeal to them if wronged by Bahima, and could not say that there was not a final human, and even supernatural arbiter of their case. However, Oberg's analysis of the practice of justice by king and Drum reveals that the structural subordination of the Bairu is reflected in it. The saying goes that, 'The Bahima are the cattle of Bagyendanwa (drum) and the Bairu are his goats.' Cattle were superior to goats in Ankole. Furthermore, it was necessary for both parties in a dispute to give king or drum gifts to get justice, and the Bahima had more wealth than the Bairu. By the use of such practices, with their surrounding magic and ceremony, Bairu might come to internalize the ideas about the correctness of their subordinate position held by the Bahima; to believe that their subordination was ordained by tradition and divine law; that they really were inferior, and that the Bahima were born to rule. They might pass on such notions to their children as they grew up. In this way the ideology of the dominant group became widespread even among the dominated, a process which Marcuse tried to show was happening in the America of the 1950s, and which we shall discuss further in chapter 5 (Marcuse, 1972). Another source of potential conflict to the Bahima was the *international structure*, external relations with other societies. If conquered, Bahima, while retaining their privileges with regard to Bairu equivalents in surrounding societies, were nevertheless temporarily impoverished, and subject to arbitrary tribute to the conquerors. The threat of invasion was real enough to the Bairu, too, since if they were captured, they had their ears cut off and became slaves, the ultimate degradation. This tended to link them to the Bahima, who, because they were the only ones to possess weapons, were the only ones who could protect them from such a fate. In fact, the continual warfare can be seen to reduce the risk of internal conflict for all the societies in the area, as the threat of slavery for all in the Bairu led them to depend on those who could provide protection against this risk. Nevertheless, the succession ritual of Ankole becomes more intelligible if seen in terms of this second source of potential conflict. Although important concessions to favouritism are made in terms of the privileged position of the favourite son, it ensured that the Bahima would be led by military leaders who had proved their worth in battle, and their ability to marshal forces by obtaining the support of sufficient Bahima allies in the internal wars. New kings had no rivals to challenge their position. The succession ritual as a whole can be understood as the attempt over the centuries of the Bahima to safeguard themselves against the external threat of invasion or raids, a threat resulting from the international organization of that area of Africa.

The provision of great power to kings involves a further potential conflict; since the supplies required to maintain kings and their entourages were partly derived from the Bahima, they might need protection from that same power themselves. If a greater physical force were set above a king, the latter would be superfluous. The only way of attempting to control the controller was therefore in the realm of ideas. As in medieval Europe the king's power was not absolute but came from God, so in Ankole the king's power came from the symbol of perfect kingship, the sacred drum, whose mystique, which everyone knew about, involved the king in custom and ceremonial. The fact that the drum, insignia of kingship, was awarded by a powerful Muhima symbolized that the king's authority came from this group, and linked the religious symbols and the structural dominance of the Bahima.

Problems of using the structural conflict approach in advanced societies

Ankole structure as described by Oberg was not too complex. Its historical development, in as far as it could be found out, gave a clear guide to the structural relationships which enable us to understand practices that had developed over the years in Ankole. This method of analysis does not assume that Ankole practices were deliberately and consciously thought out by the Bahima in order to safeguard their position, although it is not impossible that some of the practices might have been. What are the problems of applying such a method of analysis to societies such as our own? The first is the complexity of modern literate societies, as compared to societies like the Ankole. It is not a question of having too little material — inadequate written records — but too much, containing many diverse opinions. The task of singling out the key groups, and the basis, extent and development of dominance — subordination relationships between them, is not an easy one. Where reality itself is really complex, the difficulty of the problem is often increased by the fact that some sociologists seem to try to evade the need to study the complexity of reality by developing complexity of terminology instead. Their language itself becomes convoluted and tangled, as if in an attempt to parallel the problems of the real world without ever meeting them:

> The conditions of manipulative complementarity and transactional co-operation illustrate an alternative to evoking or establishing

consonance that is open for the goal originator. This alternative, of course, consists of wittingly or unwittingly 'paying off' others for becoming involved in the institutionalized pattern subserving the originating goal. For the others who become implicated in the inter-personal pattern under these conditions, the activity presents a round about route toward their own extraneous, presumably valent, specified and subjectively legitimate goals. But even assuming that these extraneous goals are unproblematic for the persons holding them, there must exist, (with certain exceptions) at least a minimal degree of consonance with respect to the originating goal, for them to become involved in the pattern directed toward it (Zollschan and Perucci, 1964).

In the last century, Engels once observed of the Hegelian school:

It . . . was limited to . . . a compilation of words and turns of speech which had no other purpose than to be at hand at the right time where thought and positive knowledge were lacking. Thus . . . these Hegelians understood nothing about anything, but could write about everything . . . These gentlemen were, in spite of their sufficiency, so conscious of their weakness that they gave big problems the widest berth possible (Engels, 1968b).

Many of the sociologists we are criticizing have hardly heard of Hegel, but otherwise the comment fits perfectly.

A second problem arises from sociologists, membership of societies they are analysing. It is difficult for someone who is part of something to stand *apart* from it, and analyse it as a whole (Elias, 1956). All of us are bound up in the beliefs and ways of thinking we have absorbed since our childhood. This pressures us towards looking at problems in certain ways, and tending to disregard other ways. It means that our personal relations, even our jobs, are involved in the kind of thinking we do — problems that were examined in the first chapter. It would be the greatest of mistakes, however, to believe that there is only one unified way of thinking in our society, as there often was in un-developed societies such as the Arapesh. There are many traditions and sources to choose from, even if, among different groups at different times, some are more popular than others.

The third, and perhaps the major problem about the application of dynamic structural conflict analysis, to our societies, is that such analysis involves us in the great political and social issues of the day. It involves us in the attempt to analyse, as carefully as we can, problems about which there may be systematic or non-systematic distortions in terms of available information; problems the investigation of which may be felt by powerful groups to threaten their interest. It is not difficult for us to examine the situation in Ankole dispassionately, since we are not directly involved in that society, and its forms of organization are rapidly becoming a part of history. But imagine the effect of the publication of such an analysis in Ankole itself, in the local language, in the heyday of the social structure described. Doubtless, large sections of the Bahima would see the very publication of the analysis, the very asking of those questions, as a threat to their positions. Suppose the Bairu were to get hold of it — might the explicit recognition of their position of subordination in the society not encourage them to wish to change it? The publication of a structural analysis of Ankole society in such circumstances becomes a political act, one which would probably lead to the removal of the head of the author. There is no doubt also that, in analysing our own societies, there are social pressures to keep off the analysis of 'difficult' matters. There are pressures to confine our attention to subordinate problems — although even the analysis of subordinate problems in sociological terms depends on the use of the best available conception of the overall structure of the society. There are pressures to express ourselves in terms so abstract that no specific existing society is examined at all.

It has been frequently argued that for some or all of these reasons, structural conflict analysis is 'unscientific', and that concern should be directed to more easily manageable, small-scale problems. We have shown, on the other hand, that it is not only the best method of approaching sociological analysis, but an indispensable method.

In an historical structural analysis of our own societies some facts emerge as crucial — the relationship between what women do and what men do, the ownership of wealth of society and how it is distributed. Such analyses would certainly be central to a sociological examination of our own society; but, for all the material there is, it has not been a central research focus for our sociologists (Miliband, 1973).

This kind of research is at least necessary to the understanding of our society. It is not our job here to attempt to carry out a structural analysis of British or any other society — it would take a much larger volume. We want to explain the necessity for, and some of the principles of, such analyses, and indicate some of the reasons why they are not carried out as they should be. Perhaps one of the reasons for the appeal of functionalism and its derivatives is now clearer. Having an extra-historical, extra-social principle of analysis — the maintenance of order — functionalists are enabled to avoid the knotty problem of involvement by adopting a spurious objectivity.

Chapter four

Social change

The inadequacy of order and change as principles of analysis

If we reject some extra-social principle by which to explain social phenomena — for instance, the idea that there is some principle of order, by which all social events can be understood — we are forced instead to examine the position of social groups in social structures. This examination involves considering the groups in interaction over time, so that all sociological analysis must be, to an extent, historical and dynamic. For reasons we have already outlined, in a sociology which is dominated by functionalist types of approach, we can expect many studies that ignore this dynamic element, and indeed there are many. But they all smuggle in assumptions about the past of the events they try to account for. Since these assumptions are not examined, all such studies are fundamentally inadequate, no matter what grand pretensions to rigorous methodology they may have.

One group of writers has been critical of functionalism and its variants because, they argue, it has ignored the fact, obvious if one considers the societies of the world as a whole over the past two thousand years or so, that social change, both of subordinate parts of social structures, and of whole social structures, has been continuous and universal. Perhaps the main advocate of this view has been Ralf Dahrendorf, who sets out his criticisms in a most stimulating article, *Out of Utopia* (1964). Such writers are correct as far as they go, but they fail to challenge the logical fallacy in attributing a supra-social motive to society, the maintenance of order. They fall into the same fallacies in an opposite way, asserting that there is some mysterious thing about society which makes it change all the time, unless something stops it. Dahrendorf says:

A Galilean change of thought is required which makes us realize that all units of social organization are continuously changing, unless some force intervenes to arrest this change.

This assertion is as baseless as its opposite, but it has led many writers to suggest that there is a choice in sociology, one which depends to a considerable extent on the temperament of the student. If you are an easy-going sort of person, you will probably like an approach based on order, while dynamic, bustling people are going to prefer change. Cohen, a British writer, prefers order for four completely spurious and unexamined reasons (Cohen, 1968, p. 18, paragraph 1; examine why they are spurious). Chinoy considers a little of both to be necessary (Chinoy, 1967, ch. 5, 'Modes of Sociological Analysis' – a chapter full of all the mistakes we have been describing with regard to the use of the word society). Inkeles recognizes that different approaches alter the results, but nevertheless refuses to evaluate them (Inkeles, 1964, ch. 4, pp. 34-9).

The whole point is that any statement about order or change in a society depends on an analysis of the interactions of groups in the social structure of that society. In other words, a structural-historical analysis will enable us to explain both order and its absence and change and its absence. There are many examples of research which came to grief because of false ideas as to how to set about the task, and a lack of structural-historical approach. In one famous case, Elton Mayo and his researchers, working on the Hawthorne studies in an American factory, heard 20,000 interviews in which numerous grievances were expressed. No one criticized the management of the firm, yet the research ended in an atmosphere of bitterness as many workers at the plant were declared redundant (Horowitz, 1963; Blumberg, 1974, ch. 2, 3). More recently, a team of British sociologists who ought to have known better spent a great deal of time and effort concocting theories as to why the workers at the Vauxhall car factory were so orderly. Barely a month after the publication of the research, the plant was subject to some of the most violent strikes of the 1960s in the British motor industry (Blackburn, 1967, pp. 48-50). American sociologists have been rightly criticized for failing to predict or understand the so-called 'race-riots' (socio-economic uprisings?) in the Black ghettoes of American cities (Baran and Sweezy, 1968, ch 9; Silberman 1964), while endless volumes written to explain the stability of 'advanced', 'democratic' societies have been deflated by the events in France in May 1968 (cf. Mandel, 1968). Many studies in so-called political sociology are devoted to trying to show that we can learn significant things about politics in a society by learning the preferences of voters on day X of month Y of year Z (cf. Samuel, 1960). Incidentally, in the first Russian revolution of 1905, Leon Trotsky, its main leader, saw the circulation of his newspaper rise from 500 to 300,000 in a month (Trotsky, 1975, p. 177). In 1917, when *Pravda*, the previously banned Bolshevik newspaper, reappeared, its second issue sold 100,000 copies (Carr, 1966, p. 84). In Britain an authoritative study of race relations drew the conclusion that because an attitude survey defined most people as relatively unprejudiced against coloured immigrants, one way of undermining prejudice was to remind people that it hardly existed. What is there in such ideas to explain the re-emergence of significant fascist organizations and the widespread dissemination of fascist ideology which has occurred over the past ten years? (Rose, 1969, p. 551; Walker, 1976.) Where in all the sociology of the family written before the early 1970s was any historical structural analysis which would make sense of the re-emergence of the women's movement on such a wide scale in so many capitalist societies? A sociology which enables us to explain and predict such changes could approach a science of society; much of what passes for sociology is pseudo-science, in spite of its pretensions, because its basic approach is fallacious.

Sociologists do not need just to pay a little more attention to change, or even a lot more, nor do they need to make change, as opposed to order, their basis of analysis. Rather they need to make groups of people in interaction in social structures over time their basis of analysis. Unfortunately, many of the ideas that are common in much British and American sociology derive from static types of analysis, and are therefore themselves inadequate. This is true of current methods as well — for instance, opinion and attitude sampling by means of sample surveys may seem rigorous in design, but, since it is essentially an a-historical method, it has very limited application in scientific sociology (Cicourel, 1964). This is one of the reasons why a lot of sociological analysis parallels the complexity of social reality by the complexity of its language and does not explain it. If we are concerned with the interrelations over time of groups of people in social structures, we can describe this as studying interaction processes in structures. Since, as we shall show below, such interaction processes on a structural level almost always involve conflict and contradictions we want to call our analysis dialectical. Our argument is that using a theory of the structured dialectics of social situations, based on historical investigation, best enables people to explain such processes and predict how they will develop.

This method makes it considerably more difficult to use exact mathematical techniques in large areas of sociology, but the use of such techniques is often spurious anyway, a scientific form being substituted for a non-scientific reality. This is not to attack the use of mathematics in sociology — but to argue that the problem and appropriate method must determine what mathematical techniques can be used — not the other way round.

The title of this chapter is social change; so far, we have criticized incorrect approaches which have led, in much sociology, to under-emphasis of explanation of social change. We have showed that it is a mistake to separate change and order in such a way that one can choose to base sociological explanation on either the former or the latter. It is equally mistaken to select sometimes one type of explanation, sometimes another type, depending on whether the immediate concern is to understand why something persists or why it does not. A sociological perspective based on historical structural analysis is necessary so that we can explain persistence, change *and* the relations between them. This approach must be dynamic, not static. Further, just as we argued previously that the behaviour of individuals or groups can only be understood within the context of social structures, so, when studying social changes, the explanation of small-scale changes in a society cannot be divorced from their relationship to the total organization of the society, as it has developed historically. The kinds of interactions which provide the major basis for the sociological explanation of structural change in societies are those in which groups in different positions in the structure come into conflict. To use jargon, conflict, realized or potential, is integral to the dialectics of social change, although it is not the sole basis of change. Let us imagine a highly simplified society, in which there are two major groups. In the first instance, the groups are not in a conflict relationship. What sources of change are there?

1. By pressure from representatives of an outside society. (This source of change — or external pressure to resist internal change — is absolutely crucial in the approach to the sub-discipline of sociology which goes by the name of the sociology of development.)
2. By necessity as a result of natural events which cannot be controlled by the groups.

3. By mutual agreement of the groups. (This does not mean that the resulting change will benefit both groups equally — one group might misjudge the implications of a change, and lose out to the other group as a result.)

Let us now suppose that a structural change has occurred as a result of either 1, 2, or 3, which puts one group in a superior structural position to the other, as defined by some verifiable criterion. We now have a new social structure.

In this social structure, the groups are in a potential conflict relationship as a result of one's structural superiority over the other. What sources of social change are there? 1, 2, 3 still exist, but there are two new ones:

4. The use by the dominant group of its superior structural position to impose change on the subordinate group (this might be by coercion).
5. The reaction by the subordinate group to its inferior position in relation to the other group.

An examination of most of the world's societies shows that they approximate more to the latter type of social structure, though their structures are usually much more complex than in this simple example, and changes 1, 2, 3 more often than not lead away from non-conflict-based structures towards conflict-based structures. We are therefore justified in concluding that conflict, which is implied by 4 and 5, and usually by 1 as well, is integral to social change, as we asserted above. Notice that the way that we have presented the argument seems to suggest conscious decisions by the members of the groups involved. Historical examination of societies, however, shows that this is not by any means always the case. As has been pointed out earlier, some decisions are taken consciously; some seem to the participants to 'happen', since they derive from structural pressures which people themselves don't understand, or are mystified about; some are a mixture of both; other decisions may have consequences different from those intended. Writers who argue that type 4 sources of change are conscious decisions have been scathingly labelled 'conspiracy theorists' by some sociologists. Whether a change from source 4 is wholly, or partly, due to a conspiracy among members of a dominant group can only be determined by the actual study of the circumstances involved, which is often very difficult. Groups who do not wish it to be known what they are deciding are hardly likely to be frank with sociologists or to leave easily available records (Mills, 1959a, part 1).

Here is an example of a study of social change. The example comes from social anthropology, for the same reasons as before, namely, that it is less complex in some ways than the study of our own society, and also because we are less involved in it. Kathleen Gough studied changes in family relationships among the Nayars of the Malabar coast of India (Gough, 1952). The basis of her study is not merely interviews with villagers from the area, but a careful examination of written records about this society, dating as far back as the sixteenth century.

The Nayars live on the south-west Indian coast, part of the population of the area known as the Malabar coast. They were a caste grouping in the kingdoms of Calicut and Cochin, i.e., a group of the population recruited by birth. Their distinctiveness was based on the general type of occupations they held, and sanctioned by religious beliefs and practices which had grown up over a long period. (For additional discussion of caste, see among others Cox, 1970, part 1.) The organization of the Nayar family was based on a family group, centred on the mother. Property and inheritance came through the mother and not through the father, whose property, etc., went to his sister's children. This kind of family system anthropologists call a matrilineal kinship system, and it has the effect of weakening relationships between the family created by marriage, and strengthening those on the mother's side of the family a person is born into. Also, the Nayars were both polyandrous and polygynous. That is, a woman normally had several husbands, and a man several wives. If a man were staying with one of his wives for the night, he would leave his weapons outside her door, to indicate to her other husbands, of whom there might be seven or eight, that he was within. Husbands had very few obligations to their wives, who were supported by their maternal family group. The paternity of children was usually uncertain, and divorce was a mere formality. In addition to these tenuous husbands, a woman was ritually married to one of an appropriate group of Nayar men when she was very young, although this ritual marriage gave the husband neither obligations to her, nor rights over her. It simply established a woman's eligibility for other husbands. The problem for sociologists is to explain the reasons for this interesting family system, and its subsequent changes. Gough searches for explanation in the development of the structural organization of the kingdoms where the Nayars lived, and their relations with surrounding societies. Over a period of time, as a caste system of society develops, a group of the population becomes specialized in a type of occupation. Their specialization becomes hereditary, so that a person cannot marry someone from another caste − a fisherman could marry a fisherman's daughter, for example, but never a pot maker's daughter. The system is also hierarchical, so that some jobs are, in belief and religion, better than others, and worthy of more social reward. The dangers of protest and revolt by those who suffer under this system at the expense of those at the top are mininized by the theology, which teaches that a good, obedient member of a low caste may be reborn into a higher caste, but that someone who protests may find themselves reborn as an animal or insect. Analogous justifications in our society come from preachers who tell us that if we happily bear our lot in this world, we shall be rewarded in the next. Since people in all castes were taught to believe the Hindu version implicitly from childhood, it provided a very effective means of resisting change, especially since the caste trained in the use of weapons was near the top of the hierarchy. The Nayars were such a military group. But in a caste system, to have a hereditarily based military group creates certain problems, for, if warriors become too attached to their wives and children, they may not be so keen to fight. On the other hand, they are the only source of new warriors, since no woman from the military caste may have intercourse with someone from outside the caste. It is very likely indeed that the Nayar family system developed as a solution to this problem. Through the maternal family group, mothers could be provided for and children brought up, while older men and women, as well as tenant serfs, could cultivate lands collectively belonging to the group. The multiple husband–wife marriage system meant that a man could father children, or satisfy sexual desires, without having any strong obligations either to his wife or to his children which might have made him reluctant to fight. This view is strengthened by the fact that in adjacent northern kingdoms where Nayars fought only intermittently for different chiefs and owned their land, polyandry was unknown.

At the end of the eighteenth century, British controlled forces with superior organization and weaponry conquered the Rajah's armies, and imposed British rule over the area. In terms of our previous discussion, a source one change took place. The Rajah's armies were disbanded, the Nayar soldiers returned to their family groups, and soon the polyandrous system of Nayar marriages died out, indicating its close link with the Nayars' structural position. It would be a mistake to explain this change in purely military terms, however. The British acted neither from a desire to show their military might, nor from a wish to 'civilize the natives', but because political control made the export of India's wealth to Britain easier. In the fifty years between 1750 and 1800, between £100 and £150 million at least of India's wealth was transferred to Britain, wealth which was an important help in providing the capital necessary for Britain's industrial revolution in the nineteenth century (Mandel, 1972, p. 443).

As the young Nayar men returned home and began to cultivate their fields themselves, they were more around their wives and children, which subjected them to conflicting loyalties between their own children and those of their sisters; between their own wives, and the demands of their maternal relatives. Since the matrilineal system was now no longer related to the Nayar's position in the social structure, the conflict was between the new position of the Nayar males, and old traditions and customs, which slowly began to decline. As the century went on, the British introduced roads and railways, so that British goods, now being produced in huge quantities in the North of England could be easily sold, incidentally destroying the local handicraft production of India, and underdeveloping India into a backward country (Barratt-Brown, 1970, pp. 41f., 174f.). At the same time, plantations for tea, coffee, and rubber were opened up by the Europeans so that the natural wealth of the land could be exported. Labour for these jobs was not recruited on a closed caste basis, and cash wages, small as they were, meant that a money economy increased in importance. Since the Nayars' matrilineal family system was linked to the caste system, as the caste system was eroded, so the decay of the family system was speeded up. Through the nineteenth and early twentieth centuries, the nuclear family (father, mother, children) was developing at the expense of the matrilineal family group.

This example illustrates several important points. First of all, the key to understanding the changes that took place within the Nayar family lies in the effects on the local social structure of a source one change, the British intervention. Second, the changes in the Nayar family system were not intended or planned by the British — they were an indirect result of the British satisfying their economic interests at India's expense (although not all Indians suffered equally — as is often, indeed usually, the case, those in subordinate positions in the social structure suffered most). Third, the major explanation of the changes cannot be found in the influence of European ideas — about monogamy, or the inheritance of property from father to son, for example, Gough is careful to point out, that other European ideas, Christianity, for example, had almost no impact on the Nayars. Thus, in this case, an *idealist* explanation of the changes is not upheld (in sociology, idealism is used to mean a theory which explains things as being caused by ideas).

Approaches to the study of social change

We are now in a better position to examine some of the approaches to the explanation of social change which are current in sociology, using, where appropriate, examples and models we have already introduced into the text (Gerth and Mills, 1970, ch. 13 is useful for reference here). As we pointed out at the beginning of the book, the extent to which this subject is studied at all, especially at introductory level varies from country to country and school to school of sociology. Since we have shown that there is no separate study of social change, no separate subject at all, the discussion ought to be part of basic sociology. If you agree, but it isn't on your course, find the reason why.

In explaining the reasons for the disappearance of polyandrous marriage among the Nayars, Gough gives weight to one factor – the disbanding of the Rajah's armies by the imposition of British control. Explanations of social change which stress one factor are often called *monistic*, while theories of social change which say that all social change is due to one factor are called monistic theories. Suppose Gough had tried to list every possible factor in accounting for the disappearance of polyandry. Probably the list would have been very long. An attempt to explain social change in terms of numbers of factors is called pluralistic. The distinction between monistic and pluralistic is therefore worth examining in more detail, because there have been a lot of arguments about whether explanations in terms of one factor are of any value. As is often the case, the easiest way to sort out the problem is to take a hypothetical example.

Hypothetical example

Imagine three social changes. We can call them X, Y, and Z. Let's start by trying to explain social change X. Let us suppose that we can get a 100 per cent explanation by using five factors, *a, b, c, d, e. a* accounts for 80 per cent of the explanation, and *b, c, d, e,* for 5 per cent each.

In explaining social change Y, on the other hand, *a* accounts for 50 per cent, *b* for 30 per cent, *c* and *d* for 8 per cent each and *e* for only 4 per cent.

In explaining social change Z, each of the five factors, *a, b, c, d, e* accounts for 20 per cent.

So each of the changes has a different *kind* of explanation. For social change X, if we explained it *monistically*, using factor *a* alone, we would still have a good explanation, though not a perfect one. For social change Y, if we used factor *a* alone, we should have a reasonable explanation and we would have picked out the most important factor. If we used factors *a* and *b*, we would have a good explanation which used the two main factors. For social change Z, we would have to have at least three factors to get a reasonable explanation, and even if we had four, we should still be ignoring another main factor.

Obviously, considering how difficult sociological research is, monistic explanation would be very satisfactory in cases like X. In cases like Y it would be satisfactory and a two factor explanation very satisfactory. In cases like Z, only a *pluralistic* explanation would do. It is therefore nonsense for sociologists to assert that only pluralistic explanations of social change will do, unless most social changes in the real world are similar to type Z. In fact it is much more correct, in terms of all the research that has been done, to say that most explanations of social change resemble X and Y. So it is wrong to assert that pluralism is necessary for the reasonable explanation or prediction of most social changes.

So far, our hypothetical example has been presented statically, as if all the explaining factors were separate. It is more difficult, but a better approximation to reality, to imagine the example with the factors in interaction over time. Let us take social change Y. Factor *a* was 50 per cent, $b - 30$ per cent, c and $d - 8$ per cent and $e - 4$ per cent in terms of their contribution to the total explanation of the change. If we introduce a time factor, *a* must be expressed as the composite factor *a*, the result of (*a* influenced by *b*, *a* by *c*, *a* by *d*, *a* by *e*), composite factor *b*, the total of (*b* influenced by *a*, *b* by *c*, *b* by *d*, *b* by *e*), and so on. This will also be true for social change Z. In other words, the 'true' isolated factors disappear, and what we have are factors 'contaminated' by other factors. In reality, the 'true' factors never occur, so all factors are 'contaminated' ones. But there is still an important difference between social changes Y and Z. In the case of Z, all the interactions will be of equal explanatory importance. In the case of Y, the influence of factor *a* on factor *c* will be greater than that of *c* on *a*, and so on. In the latter case, some interactions are more important than others, giving a hierarchy. Where conflict is involved, the process of interactions leading to Z is *dialectical*, but the process of interactions leading to Y is a *structured dialectic*, and we can substitute these terms for pluralism and monism respectively, in the static model.

We argued that there was no separate theory for social change and for social order. Suppose we consider some of our factors *a, b, c, d, e*, not as positive reasons for change, but as reasons for lack of it. Then

61

the result of examining the interactions will tell us whether a structural change is involved or not. For instance, let us consider X as the disappearance of polyandry among the Nayars. Factor *a* becomes the British control over the society. It is more important than factor *b*, the Rajah's control. But if the Rajah had defeated the British, polyandry would probably have continued to exist. A dialectical approach is therefore not only appropriate for the explanation of social change, but the method for all structural sociological explanation.

It is now possible to continue our examination of approaches to social change. Suppose we had 100 cases of type X or Y social changes. If in all of them, or a large proportion of them, the main explanatory factor was the same, we would begin to think that we had discovered a very important aid to our studies, for, in spite of the differences between the problems, we should have a line of approach that would be very helpful. Many social theorists have argued that no such aid exists, that every case has to be studied entirely afresh, that there are no 'laws of history' (Popper, 1960). If we were to use the word law to mean something that invariably happened as a result of something else, they would be right.

If we talk rather of trends, of guides to approach, it is much less plausible to deny that there are explanatory factors common to many social changes (Bottomore, 1977, ch. 2; Taylor, 1958; Novack, 1968). In fact, many sociologists have posited such factors, and their propositions fall into three great categories.

Into the category of *idealism* fall those theories which put forward the view that the source of social changes lies most importantly in people's minds, in the sorts of ideas that they have. Auguste Comte took this view, as does David McClelland today (Mill, 1961; McClelland, 1976). It is not plausible, for if it were true, ideas would occur at random, independent of place and circumstance, and social change follow from them. As we shall see in the next chapter, and have already discussed to some extent in chapter 2, human beings are dependent on social training for the very language they use, so the absolute independence of ideas is not upheld (MacIntyre, 1967, ch. 1; Gerth and Mills, 1970, ch. 10; Frank, 1971).

Those theories which attribute the major source of change to material changes, usually of technology, we can call *mechanical materialist*. Ludwig Feuerbach took this view, and Hart and Leslie Whyte are modern representatives (Engels, 1968b; Whyte, 1949; Hart, 1969). It is true that the material world existed before people came on the scene, but once they are there, the decision to introduce any technology is a human one, though it may have unforeseen consequences. The technology *alone* cannot be considered the key explanatory factor (cf. Gerth and Mills, 1970, ch. 13).

Theories of dialectical materialism argue that a major key to the explanation of structural social change may be found in the relations that people enter into in order to produce and appropriate the wealth of a society. Marx developed this kind of approach. Some modern exponents are Baran and Sweezy (1968), Frank (1973), Mandel (1972) and Bravermann (1974). This kind of theory is structural and sociological, but, if misapplied can end up as a sort of dogmatics, providing a mechanical formula by which every social change is explained, without the need to study at all. This kind of distortion has often been called economic determinism, or 'vulgar marxism', and has been practised on a large scale by so-called Marxists, most notably those connected with the bureaucratically based elites of the Soviet Union (Marcuse, 1968b). In the context of the cold war, and given that Marx's theories predict the downfall of those groups now controlling our societies, it has been widely propagated that dialectical materialism means economic determinism. Many people have come to accept such distortions. They are not correct. The reader is invited to read two articles by Marx, *The Civil War in France*, and *The Eighteenth Brumaire of Louis Napoleon,* to see how he applied dialectical materialism (Marx, 1968). Engels, Marx's close collaborator, wrote:

> The economic situation is the basis, but the various elements of the superstructure — the political forms of the class struggle and its results: to wit constitutions established by the victorious classes after a successful battle, etc., juridical forms, and then even the reflexes of all these actual struggles in the brains of the participants, political, juristic, philosophical theories, religious views, and their further development into systems of dogmas — also exercise their influence upon the course of the historical struggles, and in many cases preponderate in determining their form (Engels, Letter to Bloch in Marx and Engels, 1968).

A careful formulation of dialectical materialism has been made by Althusser (1967). Although the language is difficult, it repays study because, instead of just paralleling the complexity of the real world, it does help us to understand it. To emphasize that dialectical materialism is not simple economic determinism, Althusser introduces the idea of *overdetermination*. This combines two propositions: (1) no factors of explanation can be isolated from their social structural context; (2) although the examination of relationships of production and appropriation of wealth is crucial, it is unlikely by itself to be adequate to a proper explanation of social change. He considers how such factors both determine and are determined, 'in one and the same movement by the various levels and instances of the social formation'; 'The economy is determinant (of social change) but only in the last instance'; however, 'The lonely hour of the "last instance" never comes.'

His argument is for detailed study of the whole situation in historical perspective in order to determine the major factors and the way they interrelate. It is equivalent to saying in the terms we have used above, that most social changes are of type Y, rather than of type X or Z. Althusser illustrates his approach by an analysis of the Russian revolution, indicating the overdetermining factors on which it depended.

More recently the re-emergence of the women's movement has brought fresh criticisms of dialectical materialism, especially in its determinist versions. These criticisms point to the blatant neglect of women particularly in twentieth-century marxism (Mitchell, 1971, ch. 4) and the limitations and distortions both of social analysis and of social practice which result from this. Whether theories which focus on the significance of the mode of production can be reformulated to take account of these critiques is itself a matter of debate amongst feminists. Some of us argue that it can (Eisenstein, 1979; Hamilton 1978; Kuhn and Wolpe, 1978). Others argue that a new theory is necessary, in which the concept of patriarchy is a central one, insisting that the production of people, which has been women's central task through history, cannot be reduced to the production of things. Available evidence from both historical and social anthropology suggests that the subordination of women pre-dates property relationships, and various writers are beginning the task of working out the implications of this (Chodorow, 1978; Coulson, 1978; Delphy, 1977; Firestone, 1973; Gough, 1975; Millett, 1971; Riddell, 1978).

These approaches are the most significant attempts to provide a way in to the study of social change, by searching out the most crucial general factors. It is clear from the text that we think such an attempt is valuable, and which approaches we favour. But it is very important to understand that the merits of such approaches cannot be decided *a priori*; they derive from, and must be judged by, the examination of social reality. Since these approaches are expressed in such broad terms, they cannot be refuted in any simple way. Because of the complexity of most social phenomena, it is often possible for investigators to single out those factors which seem to lend weight to the approach which they consciously, or subconsciously hold. As the political implications of different approaches are also intertwined with all this, it becomes easy to understand why there is disagreement among sociologists. In the end, students have to make judgments for themselves. In our view, a good way of reaching such judgments is to compare studies of similar social problems by different approaches, examining their logical construction, and their use of evidence.

Among other methods of trying to study social change, two should be mentioned since in various forms they have considerable influence. Theories which maintain that the basis for sociological analysis is the maintenance of order are logically debarred from explaining social change (Rex, 1970). In trying to square this particular circle, functionalists have come up with the concept of 'structural differentiation', of which Neill Smelser has been the main proponent (Smelser, 1960). This shows that the functions which one institution performs come, over time, to be spread among other institutions – differentiated. It is argued that one form of social equilibrium is replaced by another, more complex one, with possibly a period of tension, disturbance in between. This approach is a prime example of a fault commonly found in studies of social change – it does not really explain what is happening, but merely describes it in a different way, so that a sleight of hand is involved. There is the appearance of an explanation, but really, none is given. The method is also static, moving from one 'equilibrium' to another. When one asks for the reasons for the initial situation, and the reasons for the changes – why? questions – the whole façade collapses. Smelser's main example is change in the cotton industry in the British industrial revolution. The reader is invited to compare it with a dialectical materialist interpretation by E. P. Thompson, remembering that the latter writer is an historian, not a sociologist, and thus tends not to lay out his principles of analysis explicitly (Thompson, 1970).

There is a vast amount of literature on the sociology of 'development' – the study of underdevelopment, which contains a large amount of the poorest writing in sociology, and some of the best. A common theme in this literature is that of 'modernization'.

Writers from an 'advanced' society, usually Americans, try to explain why an underdeveloped society is not like their own, or how it might become more like their own (e.g. Lerner, 1965, among many others). Such approaches involve a basic sociological fault called *ethnocentrism*, that is, they judge another society or group by standards and practices current in their own. That underdeveloped societies have a history, a dynamic structure is ignored. These structures have in fact been affected, often for centuries, by interactions of an international nature. But such obvious and basic evidence is not taken into consideration. In no area of sociology is ideological commitment so powerful a determinant of scholarship as this. Frank has examined the field in a brilliant and devastating article, 'The Sociology of Development and the Underdevelopment of Sociology' (in Frank, 1971. See also Rhodes, 1968).

In this chapter, we have put forward the view that the study of social change is not an appendage, tagged on to the 'main study', nor that it is *the* principle by which societies should be examined. Rather since historical structural analysis provides the sociological approach which explains change and order, our material develops naturally out of the previous chapter. We argued for the necessity of a dynamic, rather than a static approach, and an appropriate language. We showed the close relationship of structural conflict to structural social change, attacked pluralism as a principle, while defending a structural dialectic approach and, in discussing key factors, support dialectical materialism and theories of patriarchy. The key area remaining is the relationship between structure and human action. It is under the heading of 'social consciousness' that we propose to examine this.

Chapter five

Social consciousness

Social consciousness and social structure

The following incident is recounted in Tom Johnston's wonderful *History of the Working Classes in Scotland*:

> At Ballindalloch, on the Spey, a poor man had been sentenced to death, and the gallows not being ready he was put in the baron's pit while the scaffold was being erected. At length everything was in order, and the baron's men called upon the prisoner to come up; but instead of coming up the doomed man drew a sword and threatened to slay the first individual who came down for him. Persuasion and threat were equally unavailing, until at last, the victim's wife appeared and cried: 'Come up quietly and be hangit, Donal', and dinna anger the laird' (Johnston, 1929, p. 47).

For Donal's wife, clearly the peace of mind of the laird meant more than her relationship to Donal'. (Perhaps the laird's oppression seemed no worse than his!) At the opposite pole, the fighters of the National Liberation Front of the southern part of the poor peasant country of Vietnam for several years kept at bay, and defeated the forces of the world's most powerful nation, the USA, forces which comprised 42 per cent of its entire land forces, 58 per cent of its marines, 32 per cent of all its fighter planes, 60 per cent of its aircraft carriers, which dropped 64,000 tons of bombs a month, and involved an expenditure of some 97,000 million dollars in the four years 1965–8. At the time some people argued that these successes were due to terrorism. In fact, they were the result of a degree of determination and conviction which can rarely have been matched in world history. This struggle also had many considerable repercussions on the political consciousness of many groups of people in the West (Therborn, 1968; Eisen-Bergmann, 1975). The toll of the war, the political protest it produced and then its defeat have been a watershed in American political and social life. In either example, the *way* in which structural conflicts are worked out depends on the *consciousness* of the participants. This is always the case.

In some cases this has led to an abandonment of sociologists' concern with questions of wider social structure altogether (Atkinson, 1972). This development revived interest in the work of G. H. Mead, an American social psychologist who emphasized the importance of the interactions of people in small face-to-face groups in developing the images which people have of themselves, of others, and of society generally. It has given life and careers to the practitioners of such 'sub-fields' as interactionism, social interactionism, dramaturgy, phenomenology, ethnomethodology, etc. Erving Goffman has been influential in this development, exploring how people manage their appearances in face-to-face encounters, and the individual adaptations people make within large-scale — and often oppressive — institutions. He is interested in non-verbal as well as verbal dimensions of behaviour. Garfinkel, the 'founding father' of ethnomethodology, has probed the boundaries of assumptions which are taken for granted in conventional everyday life, which he sees as holding everyday social interactions together (Garfinkel, 1967). Garfinkel's methodology consists of exposing the boundaries of shared and taken for granted everyday meanings by transgressing them, and then observing the confused, anxious, agonized reactions of those who have been the (generally unsuspecting) victims of his method. Gouldner's criticisms of both Garfinkel and Goffman are sharp and pertinent.

> The cry of pain, then is Garfinkel's triumphal moment, it is the dramatic confirmation of the existence of certain tacit rules governing social interactions and their importance to the persons involved. ... The demonstration is the message and the message seems to be that anomic normlessness is no longer merely something that the sociologist studies in the social world, but is now something that he inflicts upon it and is the basis of his method of investigation (Gouldner, 1971, pp. 393-4).

He says of Goffman,

Goffman does not deal with how men seek to change the structures of these organizations or of other social systems, but with how they may adapt to and within them. It is a theory of the secondary adjustments that men make to the overpowering social structures that they feel must be taken as given (Gouldner, 1971, pp. 381-2).

In the peculiarly named sub-field called the sociology of deviance, the development of theories based on the examination of patterns of social interaction in the establishment of social definitions and of social meanings has been an important way of challenging the positivistic methods, assumptions, which had previously dominated the study of crime, mental illness, etc. There have been interesting investigations not into the social background of 'deviants', but into the ways in which people in other social positions create and reinforce the definition of a person as a 'deviant', even to themselves. But these investigations of how people become 'labelled' have also avoided the question of *why* this happens; by showing limited interest in the unequal power structure of society, their radical departure from positivism has been limited (Pearson, 1975). Besides, the concept of deviance often seems to imply that there is a general consensus about normality and that most people abide within it. This may or may not be the case and must itself be a matter for sociological exploration.

Many structuralist sociologists have tended to under-emphasize or even ignore the importance of people's social consciousness in determining the actual courses of events. Though this is most true of functionalists, Marx himself never gave sufficient attention to the problem. Still, he always made clear in his approach that the *consciousness* of the members of a social class belonging to that class was necessary if joint action by the class was to change a social structure. Scattered ideas in his writings provide a basis from which a structuralist theory of social consciousness might be constructed (Ossowski, 1963; Althusser, 1971; Meszaros, 1971).

Over the past fifteen years some sociologists have reacted strongly against the neglect of social consciousness in much functionalist theory, and its under-emphasis in much Marxist-oriented theory.

Some of these approaches have been useful in drawing attention to the levels of social consciousness expressed and developed in face-to-face behaviour (Berger and Luckmann, 1972). Unfortunately they tend to fall into the fallacy known as reductionism. This is expressed in the popular phrase, 'it's all in the mind', i.e., that the examination of all social phenomena can be reduced to the views of the situation held by the individual participants. In the same way that we established earlier

69

that a social structure is more than the sum of its parts, a social structure is more than the sum of the individual consciousnesses of its participants, though it is *not* a sort of collective consciousness. If we know that, say, three quarters of the people in a society hold a certain view at a particular time, this does not necessarily tell us what the social structure is. Thus we are arguing against the views: (1) that social structure totally determines social consciousness, and (2) that social consciousness totally determines social structure, and (3) that social structure and social consciousness are unrelated, independent.

The best way to describe the relationship between the two is a structural dialectic, i.e., their relationship is a process of conflicting interactions, of which the structural component is of greater weight. Marx expressed it, 'Men (sic) make history but not in circumstances of their own choosing.' In the last chapter we showed that a static model was inadequate to explain a social phenomenon. We had to have a dynamic, or dialectical model. The introduction of the idea of social consciousness brings a further complication. Social consciousness is just one of the factors to be considered in explanation; but it is also more than this, for all social phenomena involve the behaviour and interaction of people; thus social consciousness is involved in *every* social situation. While other factors may or may not be present in an explanation, social consciousness *always* is. This chapter attempts to explore some of the implications of this fact.

It is fairly easy to give examples to refute the proposition made by one leading British social theorist that social structure exists only 'in the head of the participants' (MacIntyre, 1969). King Canute showed his sycophantic courtiers that all his power and determination could not keep back the waves. In a social structure in which the organization of an adequate technology has not been developed, all people's efforts, say, to fly are doomed to failure. We previously gave an example of the difference between the demand for printing apprenticeships and the actual number, which is determined by factors outside the demand to a large extent − thus, however much the applicants desire to become printing apprentices, believe they can become printing apprentices, have the ability to become apprentices, some of them will be disappointed. However much an American believes that he has a chance of becoming President, it is clearly impossible for every American to become President. Even if the aspirant is a white male millionaire with a business background and a high position in a political party machine, his chances are very low indeed. If his skin happens to be black in colour, they are rather less than those of King Canute in keeping back the tide! However much someone believes a social structure to be unjust, or that a usurping social group should and can be overthrown, it is very unlikely that they on their own can achieve this end — unless social conditions are such that their views come to seem reasonable to a sufficient number of other people. These simple examples show that the ideas that social structure is either independent of, or totally determined by, social consciousness are implausible. But, whatever the contradictions in a social structure, there is no law that it will automatically be transformed without the conscious intervention of organized groups of the population (as some vulgar marxists have inferred), or that the social consciousness of underprivileged groups will automatically come to express coherently their position in the social structure, an even more common fallacy. Nevertheless, structural influences on position are powerful. In chapter 2 we gave an example of collective consciousness among working class people. Structurally, individual workers are in a very poor position to advance their interests on their own. They are much less powerful than individual employers. Only if they act collectively in solidarity with their fellows are they likely to make gains. Hence the fear of early employers to accept the organization of workers into trade unions, a fear still shared by many employers today. This also explains the pressures on trade union leaders from employers and state not to act in solidarity with their members, but to be mediators between workers and employers (Allen, 1966, ch. 1). Workers' structural position constantly reinforces collectivist consciousness, at least in some aspects, but many other influences, notably those of the employer-controlled mass media, are much more individualistic in orientation. Each generation of workers has, to some extent, to re-learn the experience of former ones, and the degree to which collective consciousness exists varies markedly from worker to worker and from factory to factory. Studies of workers in middle class occupations indicate that their structural position used to be such that their individual interests appeared to be best served by cultivating good relations with superiors, leading away from trade unionism, and to an extreme individualism in orientation to life. More recently, for some groups, especially in large institutions and mechanized offices, collectivism has come to seem more realistic, and middle class trade unionism has increased (Lockwood, 1966). Here, in order to make clearer what we are arguing, all these examples are presented as if they have a single explanation. In reality, they all have many causes, of which some are more important than others.

In an example also mentioned earlier, Bettleheim described the behaviour and attitudes of guards and inmates of a Nazi concentration camp. He found that not only did the guards come to regard the prisoners as sub-human vermin, to whom the most brutal behaviour was justified, but a proportion of prisoners came to accept, under the pressure, that they really were what the guards thought them to be, and behaved to each other as such. Bettleheim found that the prisoners who succumbed first and most readily to the guards' definition of them were those who neither held a deeply felt religious ideology nor had a clearly worked out philosophy of people in society; evangelical Christians and communists resisted more strongly than people whose religion was nominal or whose political affiliation nondescript. The interactions between prisoners and guards resulted in the adoption by one group of a self-image proposed by another; to understand why, however, we must know about the social structure of the camp, and about the historical development of the wider social structure, in two respects — firstly, what in the wider social structure was responsible for the narrower social structure of the camp; secondly, what features of the wider social structure, via the socialization process provided the basis for different types of attitudes among the prisoners themselves (cf. Goffman, 1970).

These examples have been used to indicate in different ways the structured dialectic of social structure and social consciousness. We can now consider other aspects of this difficult but basic relationship.

Socialization

Social consciousness depends on learning, and the term we introduced earlier with regard to this was socialization. Many sociologists, especially those who tend in one-way or another to personify society, lay great stress on a crude 'one way' conception of socialization, in which individuals learn to do 'as society tells them'.

Roles, provided by society, are learnt by individuals through the medium of family, friends, etc., enabling them to become adjusted, i.e., role-playing, members of society. One school of sociologists, commonly known as the culture-personality school, and heavily influenced by psychoanalytic theories, regard early childhood experiences as the paramount influence, so that, lacking any conception of social structure, they claim to be able to identify characteristics of a 'national character', which they relate to early socialization procedures of young children. Thus, in one study, the 'Great Russian character' is claimed to be a mixture of repression and violent outburst of aggression, deriving from the fact that Russian children are often swaddled when young (repression = being swaddled; violent outbursts = times when swaddling material is changed!). Studies in similar vein have been made of quite a number of societies. They are thoroughly misconceived (Gorer and Rickman, 1949; Kardiner, 1963). Useful critiques have been made by Orlansky (1949) and Lindesmith and Strauss (1950).

On the one-way conception of socialization a whole jargon can be built up, so that 'anticipatory' socialization occurs when a child in play 'rehearses' adult roles, and socialization can be typed, according to the generality of the roles learned (e.g., British subject, worker, steel worker, furnaceman. Cf., Musgrave, 1967; Coulson *et al.*, 1967). A deviant can then be defined as being for some reason inadequately socialized. Such individuals may give a means, otherwise denied to this kind of sociologist, of explaining social change. In exasperation at the mechanistic conception of humanity that this approach leads to, Wrong wrote an article entitled, 'The Oversocialized Conception of Man in Modern Sociology'. In this he argues that to present society–individual relations as a one-way adaptation depends on a consensus view of society: 'The oversocialized view of man (sic) is a counter-part of the over-integrated view of society' (Wrong, 1964). These two basic mistakes, which depend upon one another, make valueless much of the subordinate theorizing.

What we should be examining in a discussion of the development of social consciousness is not a one-way relationship between society and individual, but a structured dialectic. Pressures deriving from structural situations interact with the existing consciousness of individuals. While the language of interaction and process does not translate into statistical terms in the same way as the language of a static one-way model, it represents reality, and does not grossly distort it. The way such relationships can be conceptualized and studied has been shown in a lifetime series of researches about child development by Jean Piaget, which examines the development of some of the most basic components of consciousness. A child will absorb a new experience in its consciousness (*assimilation*). But since the child can only experience in terms of what it already knows, the experience will be distorted. In turn the experience will modify the existing consciousness (*accommodation*). Each new experience is *assimilated* into consciousness and consciousness *accommodates* to it. So a continuous process goes on. Some experiences may be more powerful than others, and thus force a bigger accommodation of consciousness (Piaget, 1953). For example,

73

young children may not be able to understand a family break up as to do with the relations between their parents, and may attribute it falsely to some fault of their own.

Only with this kind of approach can sociology do justice to the complexity, apparent contradictoriness, and individuality that human beings display. It is not just that sociologists have tried to explain too much by the concept of socialization; their principle of explanation has not been good enough. It has led to a general underestimation of the potentiality of human individuals for change given appropriate structural conditions, and provides a general ideological background for elitist, manipulative and conservative political views. This restricted idea of human potential is not confined to sociologists. Ruling groups tend to justify their positions by regarding the 'mass' as dull-witted and incapable of initiative, so that when people do act in resistance to various injustices, e.g. workers striking, this is interpreted as being 'engineered' by 'agitators', 'professional revolutionaries', etc. In 1969, *The Times* declared that there were special organizers working among Catholics and Protestants in the fighting in the northern part of Ireland, and that the Derry citizens' street-fighting techniques were being learned from groups of student revolutionaries who have come over from France to teach them (*The Times*, 13 August 1969).

The process of socialization in any complex social structure is such that potentialities for action and development in many directions are available to individuals, once appropriate structural opportunities are also made available. An example from a study in Poland illustrates this (Pomianowski, 1959). It has been observed from many countries that the attendance of working class people at theatres is very low, of the order of 3 per cent of the group. The more 'difficult' a play is, the less the interest. In a new steel making town, Nowa Huta, a theatre was built. The new company made no concessions to the new audience, putting on some of the world's avant-garde plays in the most avant-garde presentation. In a short time, a survey revealed 36 per cent of the population of the town as regular theatregoers; a parallel investigation in the old city of Cracow, with seven theatres and a great cultural tradition, revealed a figure of between 3 per cent and 5 per cent of the workers attending the theatre. The workers of Nowa Huta, although generally of lower educational standard than Cracow workers, came in the main from rural areas. Because of this they did not see the theatre as a place for the better off and not one for working people, a view which had become established over generations among the working class of Cracow. The point, however, is not so much that Nowa Huta

74

workers went, and Cracow workers didn't, but that Nowa Huta workers found no difficulty in appreciating and returning to see works which sometimes baffle audiences of the world's well-to-do intellectuals. A static socialization theory cannot allow for such dramatic realizations of potential, since nothing has been 'put in' by society which would make them possible.

Piaget's terminology could be adapted to a study of the development of group consciousness by Worsley, *The Trumpet Shall Sound* (1968). Worsley wanted to explain the strange phenomenon of the New Guinea islands known as the Cargo Cults. In these messianic cults, religious leaders would emerge in various tribes, preaching the end of the existing world and the arrival of a great ship or aeroplane, which would provide all believers with an abundance of the necessaries of life. Believers often ceased work and destroyed their existing goods in expectation of the arrival of Cargo. Worsley showed that this apparently irrational behaviour resulted from the assimilation of new and important events to an existing social consciousness. For the coming of white men had an immense impact in the technologically very undeveloped communities. The local inhabitants observed that the white men had tremendous power, and great wealth; their religion preached the coming end of the world (many fundamentalist Christian missions were established). But they never seemed to *work*. Since their wealth came in ships, or inland sometimes by plane, the secret of their wealth and power must lie in the Cargo. The one who could procure the mystical secret of the Cargo, by which wealth appeared without having to be created by work, was the great prophet and leader. Thus the people's consciousness was also accommodated to the incorporation of new symbols, and the adoption of elements of Christian belief. But the situation was not stable. Not only did the Cargo never come when it 'should' have, but, since Cargo cult believers did not work, the cults aroused white opposition. Attempts to suppress them were interpreted by local inhabitants as attempts to deny the secret to blacks, and some of the cults began to turn into uprisings. Worsley carefully details the constant development of events by which the local people gradually began to 'demystify' their consciousness of the situation. The cult movements in some cases finally became transformed into non-religious nationalist movements. This example indicates how group social consciousness can develop under pressure of events. It develops in ways which can only be understood by looking at a process of interactions beginning with the previous consciousness of the participants. But can we go further than this; is there any way of measuring the social consciousness of the participants, of evaluating it? Worsley correctly rejects Weber's proposition that social actions can be categorized abstractly into different types, yet his analysis has a structuralist view of the *framework* within which events took place, which does not depend solely on the social consciousness of the participants (Worsley, 1968, Appendix).

False consciousness

This is another very important reason for rejecting an approach which considers only the way people in a situation see it. It gives us no independent criterion by which to examine how they see things. Anthropological studies, as we have shown in previous chapters, are impossible without such a criterion. There is nothing special about studies of less complex societies which makes the principles for their study inapplicable when we look at our own societies. Merton discusses rain ceremonials among the Hopi Indians, for example (Merton, 1964). The participants undoubtedly believe that they bring rain. Meteorologists tell us that they do not. If we have no way of going beyond the consciousness of the participants, the matter ends there; similarly with the succession ritual of the Ankole, and so on. Merton used the terms manifest and latent function to distinguish between what the Hopi *said* was the purpose of their rain ceremonials, and what was their explanation in terms of the structure. We replaced the term function by the term explanation. It is also justifiable to describe the manifest explanation the Hopi give for their ceremonial as a form of *false consciousness.* This is not to say that it is illogical in terms of the belief systems and customs of the Hopi. Anthropologists have shown us very clearly the internal logicality of magical beliefs and the methods of their reinforcement (e.g. Evans-Pritchard, 1974). But the manifest explanation (a) doesn't produce the intended results, and (b) is less satisfactory than an alternative explanation in terms of structure. A brief discussion of the notion of false consciousness is contained in Willer and Zollschan's otherwise arid article on revolutions in Zollschan and Hirsch (1964, p. 132).

The idea of false consciousness is a useful way of beginning to look at ideologies in a structuralist sociology. The major problem is — how do we clearly identify structural conditions and conflicts in a complex social structure? Only when this has been done can we relate the consciousness of a group to a social structure. What happens if we try to apply the idea of false consciousness to conflict situations between groups?

Let's use a model of a simple social structure in which there are only two groups, similar to that introduced on page 55. In the second social structure we discussed, two groups are in a potential conflict relationship, as a result of one group's structural dominance. In the actual historical experience of the subordinate group, therefore, this will mean that the group's structural position will continually make its members feel dissatisfied. It is in the subordinate group's interests to change the structure, and in the dominant group's interests to defend it. Since social consciousness is always an important element in a social situation, anything that deflects the consciousness of members of the subordinate group from the realization of their position of structural inferiority will be advantageous to the dominant group. So will anything that provides a justification for the dominant group's position to its own members. The structural conflict is reflected in the social consciousness of the groups. The following are examples of types of false consciousness which might develop. Various writers have used terms such as *alienation*, or *mystification* to describe them.

1. The conflict may be expressed in a ritual way; e.g. women taking men's clothes for a day among the Zulu (p. 43), or the Bairu electing a mock king among the Ankole (p. 46). Such rituals may make the structural problems seem less severe.

2. There may be pressures on people to believe that the problem results from inadequacies in themselves rather than from structural causes. For example, studies of unemployment in the depression revealed that unemployed workers came to feel that their unemployment was due to their own personal inadequacies, rather than to the breakdown of the capitalist economic system, their structural cause (Bakke, 1940). Battered women often feel that they are responsible for their own ill-treatment and don't connect it to the unequal power relationship between women and men in society. It is only in the context of the women's movement that marital violence has become again recognized as a serious social problem (Martin, 1977).

3. Scapegoating. If people can be made to believe that a sub-group, usually part of a subordinate group is the cause of a problem, the real structural cause is overlooked. Thus the Jews were blamed for the crises in German society after the First World War (Neumann, 1967). White and black workers are set against each other on grounds of colour (USA) (Cox, 1970); Protestant and Catholic workers are set against each other on grounds of religion (Northern Ireland) (Gibbon, 1969).

4. There are pressures on people to believe that a situation is inevitable, 'god given', unalterable, a 'natural', 'right', or 'correct' state. For

instance, studies of political views in Britain have shown that there are many 'deference voters' – working class people who vote Tory because they have come to believe that the Conservative elite has a natural right to rule (McKenzie and Silver, 1968). Similarly, some women accepted as natural their subordinate social and economic position. Viola Klein, in her study of working women, reported: 'There is no trace of feminist egalitarianism – militant or otherwise – in any of the women's answers to our questionnaire, nor is it even implicitly assumed that women have a "right to work" ' (Klein, 1960, cited in Mitchell, 1971). Compare with the Soviet Union, where this right is definitely established in consciousness (W. Mandel, 1975).

5. There are pressures to believe that the consequence of changes will be worse than the existing state – for instance, the symbolic execution of the Bairu mock king, or De Gaulle's presentation of political alternatives to the French electorate in various referenda during the 1960s, or constant harping on fear of the 'unknown', or suggesting that unfortunate experiences of peoples in different structural circumstances are inevitable consequences of any change in this society.

6. There are pressures which induce groups to think of their existing state as better than that of other groups close to them or than their own past, thus deflecting their attention from their structurally inferior position. For instance, Runciman has carried out a study which examined inequalities with regard to wealth, status and power between working and middle class groups in the period between 1918 and 1962 (Runciman, 1966). Finding big differences persisting, he examined the *attitudes* of samples of different social classes, both from written statements and from questionnaires. The responses indicated that the groups and individuals to which the respondents referred in considering their position in relation to wealth, status and power, were those close to them socially. They saw their position as being a little better or a little worse off than that of their social neighbours, rather than considering their position in relation to the whole social structure. Runciman's work was spoiled because it lacked a concept of social structure, which led him into mistakes in his definitions of class, an inability to explain the persistence of inequality, an inadequate framework for the explanation of why people judge as they do, and a totally misconceived attempt to find a non-social means of measuring social justice and injustice.

All this needs to be amplified. Suppose, first, that the dominant group maintained its superiority over the subordinate group by force – coercion alone. Its members could believe any of the different types of explanation for their superiority, but members of the subordinate group know very well that it is force alone which keeps them down. One of the examples which approaches this type of situation is that after the American-backed coup in Chile (Prieto, 1974 for example). In such a case, the dominant group's beliefs are a justification or rationalization of their superior structural position. We may call them an *ideology* (Mannheim, 1966). Suppose, second, that a considerable number of members of the subordinate group come to believe that elements of the dominant group's ideology are true. They *internalize* the norms of the dominant group — to use jargon. The ideology thus becomes a dominant one. This will be made easier if the dominant group controls the information system, as it almost certainly will. Suppose, third, that all, or almost all of the members of the subordinate group accept the ideology of the dominant group (have internalized the dominant group's norms). In this case, the dominant group will have an ideological *hegemony*.

The more the situation nears hegemony, the less coercion will be required to maintain the status quo. In explaining the continuance of the structural dominance of one group over the other, coercion decreases in importance as we move from the first to the third situation. It is very difficult for a group to maintain dominance over another group for a long period by coercion alone. Rousseau once expressed the same thought: 'However strong a man is, he is never sufficiently strong to remain a master for ever, unless his power is transformed into Right, Obedience and Duty.' The degree of ideology, ideological dominance, ideological hegemony in a social situation has to be investigated by the sociologist. For instance, Marcuse tried to argue in his book, *One-Dimensional Man*, that the USA remains riven with structural conflict, but that a major deprived group, the white working class, has so internalized the norms of the dominant group, the industrial controllers, that their potential as agents of change has almost been eliminated, and that smaller groups, especially Black American workers, whose deprivation is more extreme, and who are excluded by definition from the ideological hegemony — since it is racist in conception — will act as agents of change, initially at any rate.

We are in no way trying to say that any of the various kinds of false consciousness which may manifest themselves in different social situations are necessarily consciously thought out attempts to jusfity or to delude a subordinate group by a dominant one.

False consciousness is certainly not always irrational. Often false consciousness may be a fairly direct reflection of the real lack of

79

alternatives presently available. For example, a mother's belief that her children are ultimately her responsibility, even when nurseries are provided or collective childcare is attempted by a group of people, isn't simply an irrational view. It may reflect the fragility of these alternatives in the long term in this society. Collectives break up; governments shut nurseries to economize. The constant pressure of the existing structures pushes towards the development of a consciousness which may in turn provide support for the structures. To transform such consciousness on any large scale requires much more than being able to imagine that things need not be as they are, although that is a necessary first step.

However, strains and tensions arising from the structurally inferior position of a group itself continue to occur, even if the social consciousness of the group is itself deflected so that no attempts to change the situation are made. In such cases, frustrations arising from structural deprivations may be *displaced*, to adopt a Freudian term, from their real structural cause on to other objects or activities. Such displacement may occur in coercion situations also, where people who are conscious of the basis of their problems can do nothing about it. There is, for instance, a tremendously high rate of theft from factories in Eastern Europe, where strikes are forbidden, and a considerable amount of industrial sabotage in Britain too (e.g., Cliff, 1974, ch. 14). Where the problem is not simply powerlessness in the face of coercion, but false consciousness, the behaviour may seem initially to be irrational, or senselessly violent. This kind of situation provides one basis for structural theories of delinquency, and to some extent, 'deviancy' in general (Taylor and Taylor, 1968). To the extent that this is true, the removal of false consciousness in such situations will affect the displaced behaviour as well. All in all, dominant groups have to work quite hard to maintain their situation, and have employed social scientists to help them (Ackroyd *et al.*, 1977; Niclaus, 1978).

In this chapter, we have tried to dispute approaches which ignore or pay only lip service to the ways in which people see the society in which they live; and also to challenge approaches which tend to view sociology in these terms alone. As an alternative we have argued that the general approach for examining relations between structure and social consciousness should be that of a process of interaction in which structure is dominant — a structured dialectic. By a critical examination of ways sociologists view the process by which individuals' social consciousness develops — their socialization — in which, as usual, we have attacked static, one-way approaches, we have been led to a classification of key processes by which social consciousness may be distorted in situations of conflict relations between groups. It may be noticed that, while in the last chapter our emphasis was on social change, we proposed that our arguments were applicable to all situations. In the latter part of this chapter, we have emphasized factors by which change is retarded, yet, once again, this approach can be applied to all social situations, not just those when change does not occur.

Chapter six

Conclusion

The need for a critical approach

In this short book we have not tried to give long lists of facts about 'the family in Britain'; or the percentage of working class children who enter university. Such facts are in some degree available if you wish to find them. On the contrary, we have been interested in the explanation of such things, the 'why' questions, the move from description to understanding, the reasons for finding out one set of facts rather than another. As this is an introductory book, we are therefore inviting students to ask the same questions of their teachers and courses. *Why* are you being taught in this or that way? This problem has two kinds of answer.

1. In the main part of the book, we have attempted to provide the basis of an answer by an examination of some of the common orientations to sociology, reserving our strongest criticism for the misconception that societies have some built-in tendency to order, the functionalist error. We have challenged this misconception on both theoretical and practical grounds because the misconception is so common in various forms, especially in British and American sociology. It is a misconception which distorts reality, diverts attention from the main problems, devalues history, and provides a terminology and approach which dehumanizes people in the interests of a crude and fallacious determinism. In making these main attacks, we have levelled criticisms at some other approaches — the opposite of functionalism, which merely substitutes change for order, and views which tend to suggest that social consciousness is the only permissible focus of attention. We have also presented the outlines of an alternative approach, which we consider to indicate

the way social reality can be scientifically studied by sociologists. This approach does not come 'out of our heads', but from reading and research. If a rough label is required, it may be called historical structuralism, or dynamic structuralism. This is because the approach makes no assumptions about any inbuilt purposes of societies (a semantic error). It requires that in order to explain why a society exhibits a particular change, a form of order, or its population some special behaviour, and to predict how such things will develop in the future, one has to study the interactions involved over time and their conflicts — to use a dialectical method.

2. As well as trying to demonstrate the fallacies of the approaches we have criticized, it is necessary also to examine *why* these fallacies have such power. This is a sociological problem. By examining it in the first chapter we hope to have shown not only something of the basis of the problems you as students face, but also to have introduced some sociological methods of analysis. Some of the explanation of why sociologists do things the way they do lies in an examination of the structural position of sociologists. Similarly, some of the reasons why all of us do the things we do lies in examination of our own structural positions. In trying to find out these reasons, we are involving ourselves in a form of introspection. If the reasons for our actions are not clear to us, or if they are in fact other than we believe them to be, we cannot be said to be able to choose how we act, to be responsible for our actions. Sociology is an area of argument within which there could potentially be a humanistic discipline which might help to increase the area of choice people have over their actions. Such a discipline might help them to find the *sources* to which they would have to go in order to change things. It might indicate some of the ways they could set about it. This would provide people with a more informed basis for action, increasing them, rather than cramping them into the deterministic straitjacket provided by explanations of how they 'fit in' to the social order (Ossowski, 1962).

Objectivity and controversy

Although the subject matter of sociology is real — the behaviour of people in societies over time — there are insurmountable problems in providing a non-controversial, objective science of sociology. A fundamental difference exists between the study of natural objects and that of humans. Stone is in no way affected by a geologist's analysis of the geological strata of which it forms a part, but human groups may be profoundly affected by a sociological study, since social consciousness, an 'intervening variable', may be changed by it. Thus, publication of a sociological analysis, however carefully arrived at, may be a political act. For example, publication in Ankole of an analysis of the structural basis of the inferiority of the Bairu in relation to the Bahima would almost certainly have lost the authors their heads. Suppose it were really the case that a complex social structure, like ours, was based on the exploitation and manipulation of some groups in the interests of others. If a sociologist published a true account of how this had developed and how it persisted, using, we should like to hope, the means we have outlined in the book, the publication itself could affect social consciousness. It would tend to decrease false consciousness. Possibly it would make subordinate groups more dissatisfied with their position and arouse the conscience of some of those in the superior groups. Even if it did not actually do this to any great extent, some might be afraid that it would have such an effect. As we write, the Conservative government is abolishing the Royal Commission on the distribution of wealth.

Then, certainly, replies to the objective analysis could be expected. They would be cleverly written in an attempt to show that the analysis was not objective, but distorted. The writers of such replies would not only be wrong, but dishonest – distorting science for political ends; they might, however, persuade people. Other writers might realize that their career advancement and security could be promoted by not offending dominant groups. They might put forward arguments that deflected attention from the analysis – that the job of sociology should be to study something else, how social order is maintained, perhaps – or that sociology does not have the technique to study major problems, and should therefore confine itself to areas where available techniques could be used – studies of opinions about sport, or of how people spend their time, and so on. Objectively means technique, they might say; How can your study be objective, since you do not use multiple regression analysis, which is really so sophisticated? Such people would not only be wrong, but cowards.

In our hypothetical example we see honest research distorted and attacked, to confuse the issue, and divert a student's mind from the real situation. But in the reality of our own societies, how do we distinguish between the honest researcher, the apologist for the status quo or the self-seeker? In the hypothetical case, we presumed to know which was the objective analysis. In our own society, how do we know who is objective, and who is furthering their own interests? We can only attack people for dishonesty if we know, and we don't. All we have are the controversies in sociology, and the conflicts in society which they reflect, in more or less distorted ways. As to how to select from among them — our views on that have been the subject of the book. One of the reasons, apart from simplicity, that we have made use of examples from anthropology is that it does not greatly affect *us* that, for instance, the Bahima exploited the Bairu, so we could make our point about structural conflict in a not too controversial way. If you have understood the point, apply it to the analysis of our own society, but do not expect your analysis to be non-controversial, even if you are convinced that it is the most informed available.

Values and involvement

The study of stones does not raise moral problems in itself; it is non-sensical to ask — *should* a stone be carboniferous or calcic? Moral problems derive from the human situation — it is meaningful to ask — *should* a social group be in a structurally inferior position to another group? The actual subject matter of sociology is the basis of moral judgments.

In our hypothetical case, we used value-laden terms — apologist and self-seeker — and have had to discard them. But sociologists' real work poses moral and political dilemmas. Is our purpose in undertaking a study objective, or is our choice subject to social pressures of the kinds we have described? This is itself a legitimate sociological problem. If we study one thing (say, voting behaviour), rather than another (say, the power structure of a society), when on the answers to the second the well-being of humanity might depend, are we not morally culpable, and are our justifications of our decision to study one rather than the other perhaps rationalizations?

Furthermore, we also have been and are being socialized as human beings, as part of a society. Are we not likely to have views and opinions, assumptions and prejudices of a non-scientific nature, and are these not likely to intrude, both in our selection of topics, and in the way we investigate them? We are led back again to the subject matter of chapter 1. Many sociologists, in spite of heavy and constant attacks from writers like Lynd (1969), Myrdal (1962), Gouldner (1963), Seeley (1963), ignore such problems in the name of trying to establish a 'science'. How could a study be made more scientific by

85

ignoring problems. Where real problems exist, which cannot be examined by a particular technique, then to ignore them means that to claim to be more 'scientific' is to be less scientific in reality. We think many sociologists in fact do make such claims.

Finally, as a human being, has the sociologist no concern for the world that is to be? Is it to develop towards the brutal totalitarian repression of 1984 (Orwell, 1970); or the smooth totalitarian manipulation of *Brave New World* (Huxley, 1969); or to stay forever as it is now (an impossibility really); or might it become a place where 'the free development of each is a condition of the free development of all' (Marx. For a potential utopia organized along these lines, see Piercy, 1979)? Since sociologists' research may be relevant in influencing what comes to be, have we not political choices to make, and may we not be judged by others on the basis of our choices? A significant task for sociology is to investigate forms of social organization which widen, not limit, the possibility of meaningful individual choice, which *widen* the horizons of people. Then decisions can be made not over people's heads, by forces which control them, but so that people are themselves in a position to decide as to their actions. Far from such a form of organization being an unchanging, conflictless utopia, only, as Marx argued, in such a society can *human* history be said to have begun (Bottomore and Rubel, 1970, part 5).

Our general point is that social reality really exists, and there is a real and important task involved in trying to understand it. But to claim that a non-controversial, value-free sociology can develop in a conflict-based social structure is theoretically untenable, practically unrealistic, and morally and politically disastrous.

Methods and problems

One of the key points of emphasis in the book has been the necessity for dialectical analysis, which we have consistently defined as the study of processes of interaction. Historical structuralism implies dialectical approaches.

Many though not all of the mathematical tools which, for various reasons, have become popular among sociologists, particularly in America, are not suited to analysis of process of interactions. Some are unsuitable for holistic analysis; a considerable number are static — that is, they depend on pretending that social reality can be 'frozen' at a particular moment. They predict by assuming that the relations between the factors measured are constant over time. The grounds for these assumptions are hardly ever spelled out, and they are quite unscientific. In theory, therefore, the whole 'scientific' basis of the work disappears. Only after examination of a problem dialectically can we make assumptions about the constancy of relations examined at any given time. One of the reasons for the popularity of theories that assume social order to be society's basic state is because they allow the use of simple statistical techniques (Irvine *et al.*, 1979).

We do not by any means oppose the use of mathematics in sociology; but we do say that the methodology of our subject is more important than the mathematics of it. Mathematics is a tool, and mathematicians must devise tools which can be meaningfully applied to dialectical analysis. This could be useful work.

In many cases, sociologists, especially those with mathematical training, have become so mesmerized by the apparent quantifiability provided by their methods that they have argued that 'scientific' sociology only exists when such techniques are applied, and that only those problems should be studied where they do apply. The mathematical techniques have come to determine the subject matter. Quantification makes a subject seem respectable. It sounds good to be able to say that 90 per cent of people think this or that at a probability level of 0.05 — until we remember that unless we understand the dialectic of social structure and social consciousness which led them to express the opinion, we haven't really a clue about how they will think or behave tomorrow, or the day after. If we spend our time studying, say, the proportion of individuals who use one product rather than another, our study will be more amenable to statistical technique than if we study the origins and development of, say, the Arab–Israeli conflict, or the development of the power structure of the Soviet Union. But the fact that statistics are easier to apply when studying behaviour in a small group at a given moment in time is no reason whatever for studying the former problem rather than the latter two. To use it as an argument distorts sociology. The student of sociology should be especially wary of 'scientism'.

Some sociologists argue that a science can only be developed by amassing small bits of information, out of which theories will emerge. But we have to make *choices* as to which bits of information to amass. Others propose that, by developing a theory of society in the abstract first, we shall be able to explain all the subordinate parts — as if the correct principles of such a general theory were 'floating' in the abstract, to be absorbed by the perceptive mind, and only had to be put together without any reference to reality at all. C. W. Mills has exposed these fallacies, which he calls 'abstracted empiricism' and 'grand theory', respectively, in his excellent book *The Sociological Imagination* (1970). What these views have in common is that they lead away from the study of social structures in historical development — one never considers the whole, the other never carries out any research. The relationship between theory and the real social world is of a dialectical nature. Ideas derived from common experience or previous study are compared with historical or present social reality. Theories are developed which are challenged, modified in application, and so on, all being subject to the sorts of distortion we have been talking about earlier in this chapter. However, if the central focus of sociology is structuralism, but few structural studies are carried out, we need not be surprised at the number of poor sociological theories that are around.

Abstracted empiricism has been closely connected with static mathematical techniques, and grand theory with the multiplication of new terms, which we have argued earlier often parallel the complexity of reality rather than explaining it. All sociologists and prospective sociologists, then, should keep firmly in mind that the proposition

Scientific Technique + Jargon = Science

while widely held is really a claim for professional recognition and status.

There are no great sociological schools in Britain (Anderson, 1969). Sociology here developed rapidly in the 1960s. Career advancement was very easy, and many sociologists quickly found it congenial to become administrators and organizers of departments. Critical students will find that much work is poor in conceptualization, abounds in logical errors, substitutes description for explanation, and assumes the answers to problems it should examine. Much research has been narrowly empiricist, based on a 'let's put all the data in the computer — something significant is bound to come out' approach. Functionalism has not the overwhelming predominance it has had in the USA, except perhaps in syllabuses for school students. Instead, there is often to be found a mild iconoclasm, part liberal, part fabian in heritage, which substitutes for a theoretical analysis. The last wave of the expansion, in the early 1970s, was associated with ethnomethodology. More recently, some circles, noting that sociology students tend to be less unquestioningly accepting of the status quo than others, have suggested that a diabolical marxism is undermining the discipline (Gould, 1977). This however, is very far from being true. In the years since we prepared the first edition of this book, more radical work has been done. Unfortunately, much of it is locked into the competitive framework of academic life so tends to be very difficult to read and understand. It reflects the elitist nature of education and its impact is thus vastly reduced.

We hope that reading this book will stimulate you to criticize the world around you and the way that it is presented through sociology. We have tried to encourage you to evaluate your course sociologically; to investigate how the controversies discussed here are presented to you, and whether they are adequately met; what principles are used in selecting facts for presentation to you; what sorts of problems are included in your studies, and why. We hope you have been provided with some basis to challenge your teachers, and encouraged to develop a critical attitude to all that you are taught. To refute them will usually require wider study — some leads can be found in the suggestions for further reading and in the bibliography. In our view, the study of sociology can be one way of beginning to ask important questions about the social world and about ourselves, but to find answers to such questions generally will take you beyond the framework of academic sociology.

Suggestions for further reading

In the text, we've given a fairly wide selection of reference to socio-logical work, representing different approaches and these are detailed in the bibliography. The suggestions which follow are not meant to be a comprehensive book list, but rather an indication of some of the writings which have influenced the development of our own perspec-tives. This list is probably even more idiosyncratic and arbitrary than that of the first edition. Since we first wrote this book, the number and range of critical studies published has increased enormously, reflecting the growth of social criticism over the past decade. Several publishers (e.g. Routledge & Kegan Paul, Macmillan), have produced series of critical studies; and several new feminist, left wing publishers have become established here (for example, Virago, the Woman's Press, Pluto Press, etc.). It is simply impossible to mention all the things that might be worth reading, but hopefully these suggestions might lead to further critical explorations.

General studies and theoretical origins

In Britain, a sociologist who has consistently produced useful and intelligible work is Bottomore. His *Sociology* (1977) and his studies *Elites and Society* (1970) and *Classes in Modern Society* (1968) remain thoughtful introductions. In addition, his translations with Rubel of Marx indicate how much maligned that great sociologist has been (*Karl Marx, Selected Writings*, 1970). A powerful American sociologist, though of quite different personality and style, was C. Wright Mills. His attacks on the prevailing orthodoxy of the 1950s, and advocacy of structuralist sociology were made in *The Sociological Imagination* (1970) and in his collected essays, *Power, Politics and People* (edited by I. Horowitz, 1963). Both his *Images of Man* (sic) (1967) and *The Marxists* (1969) were major attempts to break down parochialism. His influence can also be felt in the important critical selection edited by Stein and Vidich, *Sociology on Trial* (1963), and in Alvin Gouldner's *The Coming Crisis of Western Sociology* (1971). In theoretical terms, Althusser is an important writer. We would particularly refer to his article 'Contradiction and Overdetermination' (1967) and to his work on ideology in *Lenin and Philosophy* (1971). An examination of the origins of dialectics is provided by Marcuse in *Reason and Revolution* (1968a). Finally, a book which we consider of importance in understanding theoretical backgrounds, and which is not too difficult is E. Mandel's *Marxist Economic Theory*, as much sociology as economics (1972). His *Late Capitalism* (1975), though more difficult, is still worth while.

Critiques

It is very useful to read some critiques of commonly held viewpoints. Several of the works already referred to contain critiques; in addition, Robert Lynd's old study, *Knowledge for What?* (1969) is still as relevant as ever. Hilary Rose and Stephen Rose's collections of essays, *The Political Economy of Science* and *The Radicalization of Science* (both 1976) attempt to understand the social context and potential of science. I. Horowitz examines one aspect of the involvement of government in sociology in *The Rise and Fall of Project Camelot* (1967), as does Kathleen Gough in more general terms in 'Anthropology and Imperialism' (1968).

The student movement of the late 1960s provoked a number of attacks on conventional general sociology, which are still worth looking at. Among them, we suggest Robin Blackburn (ed.), *Ideology and Social Science* (1978). See especially Martin Niclaus's article in this. A. Cockburn and R. Blackburn (eds), *Student Power* (1969), Trevor Pateman (ed.), *Counter Course* (1972), and Martin Shaw, *Marxism and Social Science* (1975), are also useful.

Robert Young has attacked the idea of human nature and its use in social science (1973). Several critiques of Parsonian functionalism have been listed on page 37. Finally Irvine *et al.*, *Demystifying Social Statistics* (1979), examines with a critical eye methods in common use.

Particular studies

It is only by examining actual problems that you can judge any socio-logical approach. Here are just a few examples from different areas. For highly complex societies, try R. Miliband, *The State in Capitalist Society* (1973), John Westergaard and Henrietta Resler, *Class in a Capitalist Society* (1976), Carol Ackroyd *et al.*, *The Technology of Political Control* (1977), Andrew Glyn and Bob Sutcliffe, *British Workers and the Profits Squeeze* (1972), A. B. Atkinson, *Unequal Shares* (1974) (Britain). Jon Halliday and Gavon McCormack, *Japanese Imperialism Today* (1974) (Japan). C. W. Mills, *The Power Elite* (1959), P. Baran and P. Sweezy, *Monopoly Capital* (1968), Harry Bravermann, *Labour and Monopoly Capital* (1974) (USA). Rudolf Bahro, *The Alter-native in Eastern Europe* (1979) (East Europe). For countries suffering from underdevelopment, try writings by André Gunder Frank (1967, 1971, 1973), Pierre Jalee, *The Pillage of the Third World* (1970), Harry Magdoff, *The Age of Imperialism* (1969), Gerard Chaliand, *Revolution in the Third World* (1977). Specific examples are K. Gough and H. Sharma (eds), *Imperialism and Revolution in South Asia* (1973), Robin Blackburn (ed.), *Explosion in a Sub-continent* (1975) and *The Cuban Revolution* (1977), Fred Halliday, *Arabia without Sultans* (1974), and *Iran, Dictatorship and Development* (1979). For Africa we suggest Walter Rodney's *How Europe Underdeveloped Africa* (1976).

Among many powerful studies of patriarchy, we would single out Susan Brownmiller, *Against Our Will* (1976), Adrienne Rich, *Of Woman Born* (1977), Nancy Chodorow, *The Reproduction of Mothering* (1978), and Heidi Hartman's 'The Unhappy Marriage of Marxism and Feminism' in *Capital and Class*, no. 8 (1979). A powerful analysis pro-jected in science fiction is Marge Piercy's *Woman on the Edge of Time* (1979).

O. C. Cox disentangles problems of race in *Caste, Class and Race* (1970); a special study in this area is Amrit Wilson's *Finding a Voice* (1978). Examples of notable studies of social consciousness are S. Ossowski's *Class Structure in the Social Consciousness* (1963), P. Worsley, *The Trumpet Shall Sound* (1968), and William Hinton's account of the transformation of a Chinese village, *Fanshen* (1968). Good studies of education are Stephen Castles and Wiebke Wustenberg, *The Education of the Future* (1979), and Sue Sharpe, *Just Like a Girl* (1976). The Welfare State has become a focus for useful studies, e.g., Elizabeth Wilson, *Women and the Welfare State* (1977), Cynthia Cock-burn, *The Local State* (1977) and Norman Ginsberg, *Class Capital and*

Social Policy (1979). Finally, some examples of studies of social groups, Jeremy Seabrook, *What Went Wrong* (1978), Ken Coates and R. Silburn, *Poverty, the Forgotten Englishmen* (1971), Huw Beynon, *Working for Ford* (1973), Durham Strong Words Collective, *But the World Goes on the Same* (1979), Richard Hyman, *Strikes* (1972), Jill Liddington and Jill Norris, *With One Hand Tied Behind Us* (1978), Stuart Hall *et al.*, *Policing the Crisis* (1979).

Journals

It is important to look through sociological journals to examine what sort of things are being done, what sort of trends are making headway. Older established critical journals such as *New Left Review*, *Monthly Review* and *Science and Society* have been joined by many more in the last decade. These include *Economy and Society*, *Critique of Anthropology, Ideology and Consciousness, Radical America, Capital and Class, M/F, Feminist Review* among others. Also Counter Information Services and the British Society for Social Responsibility in Science put out frequent informative reports.

Bibliography

ACKROYD, CAROL, MARGOLIS, KAREN, ROSENHEAD, JONATHAN, and SHALLKE, TIM (1977), *The Technology of Political Control*, Harmondsworth, Penguin.

ALLEN, V. (1966), *Militant Trade Unionism*, London, Merlin Press.

ALTHUSSER, L. (1967), 'Contradiction and Overdetermination', *New Left Review*, no. 41, pp. 11–35.

ALTHUSSER, L. (1971), *Lenin and Philosophy*, London, Monthly Review Press.

ANDERSON, P. (1966), 'The Origins of the Present Crisis', in D. Anderson (ed.) (1966), *Towards Socialism*, London, Fontana.

ANDERSON, P. (1969), 'Components of the National Culture', in Cockburn and Blackburn (1969).

ARON, R. (1968), *Main Currents of Sociological Thought, Vol. I*, Harmondsworth, Penguin.

ATKINSON, A. B. (1974), *Unequal Shares*, Harmondsworth, Penguin.

ATKINSON, RICHARD (1972), *Orthodox Consensus, the Radical Alternative*, London, Heinemann.

BAHRO, RUDOLF (1979), *The Alternative in Eastern Europe*, London, New Left Books.

BAKKE, E. (1940), *The Unemployed Worker*, Yale University Press.

BANTON, M. (1965), *Roles*, London, Tavistock.

BARAN, P. (1973), *The Political Economy of Growth*, Harmondsworth, Penguin.

BARAN, P. and SWEEZY, P. (1968), *Monopoly Capital*, Harmondsworth, Penguin.

BARNES, H. (ed.) (1966), *An Introduction to the History of Sociology*, University of Chicago Press.

BARRATT-BROWN, M. (1970), *After Imperialism*, London, Humanities Press.

BECKER, H. (ed). (1967), *The Other Side*, London, Free Press.

BENEDICT, R. (1961), *Patterns of Culture*, London, Routledge & Kegan Paul.

94

BENOIT-SMULLYAN, E. (1966), 'The Sociologism of Emile Durkheim and His School', in Barnes (1966).

BERGER, P. (1970), *Invitation to Sociology*, Harmondsworth, Penguin.

BERGER, PETER and LUCKMANN, THOMAS (1972), *The Social Construction of Reality*, Harmondsworth, Penguin.

BERGER, P. and PULLBERG, S. (1966), 'Reification and the Sociological Critique of Consciousness', *New Left Review*, no. 35, pp. 56–71.

BETTLEHEIM, B. (1943), 'Individual and Mass Behaviour in Extreme Situations', *Journal of Abnormal and Social Psychology*, pp. 417–52.

BEYNON, HUW (1973), *Working for Ford*, Harmondsworth, Penguin.

BIDDLE, B. and THOMAS, E. (1966), *Role Theory: Concepts and Research*, New York, Wiley.

BIRNBAUM, N. (1958), 'Social Constraints and Academic Freedom', *Universities and Left Review*, no. 5, pp. 47–52.

BLACK, M. (ed.) (1976), *The Social Theories of Talcott Parsons*, University of Illinois Press.

BLACKBURN, R. (1967), 'The Unequal Society', in Blackburn and Cockburn (1967).

BLACKBURN, R. (1969), 'A Brief Guide to Bourgeois Ideology', in Cockburn and Blackburn (1969).

BLACKBURN, ROBIN (ed.) (1975), *Explosion in a Sub-continent*, Harmondsworth, Penguin.

BLACKBURN, R. (1977), *The Cuban Revolution*, London, Humanities Press.

BLACKBURN, ROBIN (ed.) (1978), *Ideology and Social Science*, London, Fontana.

BLACKBURN, R. and COCKBURN, A. (eds) (1967), *The Incompatibles*, Harmondsworth, Penguin.

BLUMBERG, P. (1974), *Industrial Democracy: The Sociology of Participation*, London, Schocken.

BOTTOMORE, T. (1968), *Classes in Modern Society*, London, London House.

BOTTOMORE, T. (1969), *Critics of Society*, London, Allen & Unwin.

BOTTOMORE, T. (1970), *Elites and Society*, Harmondsworth, Penguin.

BOTTOMORE, T. (1977), *Sociology*, London, Allen & Unwin.

BOTTOMORE, T. and RUBEL, M. (eds) (1970), *Karl Marx, Selected Writings*, Harmondsworth, Penguin.

BRAVERMANN, HARRY (1974), *Labour and Monopoly Capital*, London, Monthly Review Press.

BROOM, L. and SELZNICK, P. (1973), *Sociology*, New York, Harper & Row.

BROWNMILLER, SUSAN (1976), *Against Our Will*, Harmondsworth, Penguin.

BURRIS, BARBARA (1971), 'The Fourth World Manifesto', in *Notes from the Third Year*, ed. A. Koedt, New York, Notes from the Third Year.

CAPLOW, T. and MCGHEE, R. (1961), *The Academic Marketplace*, New York, Science Editions.

95

CARMICHAEL, S. (1968), *Black Power – Address To Congress*, London, Institute of Phenomenological Studies, Long playing record, D.L. 6,

CARR, E. (1966), *The Bolshevik Revolution, 1917–1923. Vol. I*, Harmondsworth, Penguin.

CASTLES, STEPHEN and WUSTENBERG, WIEBKE (1979), *The Education of the Future*, London, Pluto Press.

CHALIAND, GERARD (1977), *Revolution in the Third World*, Sussex, Harvester Press.

CHINOY, E. (1967), *Society*, New York, Random House.

CHODOROW, NANCY (1978), *The Reproduction of Mothering*, California University Press.

CICOUREL, A. (1964), *Method and Measurement in Sociology*, London, Collier-Macmillan.

CLIFF, T. (1974), *State Capitalism in Russia*, London, Pluto Press.

COATES, KEN and SILBURN, R. (1971), *Poverty, the Forgotten Englishman*, Harmondsworth, Penguin.

COCKBURN, A. and BLACKBURN, R. (eds) (1969), *Student Power*, Harmondsworth, Penguin.

COCKBURN, CYNTHIA (1977), *The Local State*, London, Pluto.

COHEN, P. (1968), *Modern Social Theory*, London, Heinemann.

COHN-BENDIT, D. *et al.* (1969), 'Why Sociologists?', in Cockburn and Blackburn (1969).

COSER, L. and ROSENBERG, B. (eds) (1964), *Sociological Theory*, London, Collier-Macmillan.

COTGROVE, S. (1975), *The Science of Society*, London, Allen & Unwin.

COULSON, M. *et al.* (1967), 'Towards A Sociological Theory of Occupational Choice – A Critique', *Sociological Review*, vol. 15 (3), pp. 301–9.

COULSON, MARGARET (1972), 'Role: A Redundant Concept in Sociology?', in J. A. Jackson (ed.), *Role*, Sociological Studies 4. Keele, Sociological Review Press.

COULSON, M. (1978), 'Patriarchy's Story', *Socialist Challenge*, 26 January.

COUNTER INFORMATION SERVICES (1979), *The New Technology*, London.

COX, O. (1970), *Caste, Class and Race*, London, Monthly Review Press.

DAHRENDORF, R. (1964), 'Out of Utopia', in Coser and Rosenberg (1964).

DELPHY, CHRISTINE (1977), *The Main Enemy*, London, Women's Research and Resources Collective.

DENNIS, N. *et al.* (1969), *Coal Is Our Life*, London, Tavistock.

DEUTSCHER, I. (1974), *The Unfinished Revolution*, London, Oxford University Press.

DURHAM STRONG WORDS COLLECTIVE (1979), *But the World Goes on the Same – changing times in Durham Pit Villages*, Tyne & Wear, Strong Words.

DURKHEIM, EMILE (1964), *The Division of Labour in Society*, Chicago, Free Press.

DURKHEIM, EMILE (1970), *Suicide*, London, Routledge & Kegan Paul.

EISEN-BERGMANN, ARLENE (1975), *Women of Vietnam*, San Francisco, People's Press.

EISENSTEIN, ZILLAH (ed.) (1979), *Capitalist Patriarchy and the Case for Socialist Feminism*, London, Monthly Review Press.

ELIAS, N. (1956), 'Problems of Involvement and Detachment', *British Journal of Sociology*, vol. VII, pp. 226f.

ENGELS, F. (1968a), *Karl Marx, A Contribution to the Critique of Political Economy*, in Marx and Engels (1968).

ENGELS, F. (1968b), *Ludwig Feuerbach and the End of Classical German Philosophy*, in Marx and Engels (1968).

EVANS-PRITCHARD, E. (1974), *Witchcraft, Oracles and Magic Among the Azande*, Oxford, Clarendon Press.

FIAMENGO, A. (1967), *Osnove Opće Sociologije (Elements of General Sociology)*, Zagreb, Narodne Novine.

FIELD, FRANK (ed.) (1979), *The Wealth Report*, London, Routledge & Kegan Paul.

FIRESTONE, SHULAMITH (1973), *The Dialectic of Sex*, St Albans, Paladin.

FORTES, M. and EVANS-PRITCHARD, E. (eds) (1961), *African Political Systems*, London, Oxford University Press.

FOSS, D. (1963), 'The World View of Talcott Parsons', in Stein and Vidich (1963).

FRANK, A. (1967), *Capitalism and Underdevelopment in Latin America*, London, Monthly Review Press.

FRANK, A. (1971), *Latin America, Underdevelopment or Revolution*, London, Monthly Review Press.

FRANK, A. (1973), *Lumpenbourgeoisie and Lumpenproletariat*, London, Monthly Review Press.

FRANKENBERG, R. (1970), *Communities in Britain*, Harmondsworth, Penguin.

GARFINKEL, HAROLD (1967), *Studies in Ethnomethodology*, Englewood Cliffs, NJ, Prentice-Hall.

GERSONI-STAVN, D. (ed.) (1974), *Sexism and Youth*, New York, Bowker.

GERTH, H. and MILLS, C. (1970), *Character and Social Structure*, London, Routledge & Kegan Paul.

GIBBON, P. (1969), 'The Dialectic of Religion and Class in Ulster', *New Left Review*, no. 55, pp. 20–41.

GIDDENS, A. (1965), 'The Suicide Problem in French Sociology', *British Journal of Sociology*, vol. XVI (1), pp. 3–18.

GIDDENS, A. (1966), 'A Typology of Suicide', *European Journal of Sociology*, vol. 7 (2), pp. 276–95.

GIDDENS, A. (1968), 'Power in the Recent Writings of Talcott Parsons', *Sociology*, vol. II (3), pp. 257–72.

GINSBERG, NORMAN (1979), *Class Capital and Social Policy*, London, Macmillan.

GLUCKMAN, M. (1944), *Malinowski's Sociological Theories*, London, Oxford University Press.

GLUCKMAN, M. (1955), *Custom and Conflict in Africa*, Oxford, Blackwell.

GLYN, ANDREW and SUTCLIFFE, BOB (1972), *British Workers and the Profits Squeeze*, Harmondsworth, Penguin.

GODELIER, M. (1967), 'System, Structure and Contradiction in Capital', in Miliband and Saville (1967).

GOFFMAN, E. (1969), *Where the Action Is*, London, Allen Lane, The Penguin Press.

GOFFMAN, E. (1970), *Asylums*, Harmondsworth, Penguin.

GOFFMAN, E. (1971), *The Presentation of Self in Everyday Life*, Harmondsworth, Penguin.

GOODE, W. (1964), *The Family*, Englewood Cliffs, NJ, Prentice-Hall.

GORER, G. and RICKMAN, J. (1949), *The People of Great Russia*, London.

GOUGH, E. K. (1952), 'Changing Kinship Usages in the Setting of Political and Economic Change among the Nayars of Malabar', *Journal of the Royal Anthropological Institute of Great Britain and Ireland*, vol. XXXII, pp. 71–87.

GOUGH, E. K. (1968), 'Anthropology and Imperialism', *Monthly Review*, vol. 19 (11), pp. 12–27.

GOUGH, KATHLEEN and SHARMA, HARI (eds) (1973), *Imperialism and Revolution in South Asia*, London, Monthly Review Press.

GOUGH, KATHLEEN (1975), 'The Origin of the Family', in Rayner Reiter (ed.), *Towards an Anthropology of Women*, London, Monthly Review Press.

GOULD, JULIUS (1977), *The Attack on Higher Education: Marxist and Radical Penetration*, London, Institute for the Study of Conflict.

GOULDNER, ALVIN (1963), *Anti-Minotaur. The Myth of a Value Free Sociology*, in Stein and Vidich (1963).

GOULDNER, ALVIN (1971), *The Coming Crisis of Western Sociology*, London, Heinemann.

GOULDTHORPE, J. and LOCKWOOD, D. (1963), 'Affluence and the British Class Structure', *Sociological Review*, vol. II, pp. 133–63.

GROSS, L. (ed.) (1967), *Symposium on Sociological Theory*, London, Harper & Row.

GROSS, N. *et al.* (1958), *Explorations in Role Analysis*, New York, Wiley.

GROSSMAN, RACHAEL (1979), 'Women's Place in the Integrated Circuit', *Southeast Asia Chronicle*, PSC Issue, IX (5–6).

HALL, STUART *et al.* (1979), *Policing the Crisis*, London, Macmillan.

HALLIDAY, FRED (1974), *Arabia without Sultans*, Harmondsworth, Penguin.

HALLIDAY, FRED (1979), *Iran, Dictatorship and Development*, Harmondsworth, Penguin.

HALLIDAY, JON and MCCORMACK, GAVON (1974), *Japanese Imperialism Today*, Harmondsworth, Penguin.

HAMILTON, ROBERTA (1978), *The Liberation of Women*, London, Allen & Unwin.

HAMMERSLEY, M. and WOODS P. (1976), *The Process of Schooling*, London, Routledge & Kegan Paul.

HART, H. (1969), 'Social Theory and Social Change', in Gross (1967).

HARTMAN, HEIDI L. (1979), 'The Unhappy Marriage of Marxism and Feminism. Towards a more Progressive Union', *Capital and Class* (8), pp. 1–33.

HINTON, W. (1968), *Fanshen*, London, Merlin Press.

HOROWITZ, I. (ed.) (1963), *Power, Politics and People*, London, Oxford University Press.

HOROWITZ, I. (1967), *The Rise and Fall of Project Camelot*, Massachusetts, MIT Press.

HOROWITZ, I. (1968), *Professing Sociology*, Chicago, Aldine.

HORTON, P. and HUNT, C. (1976), *Sociology*, London, McGraw-Hill.

HOSELITZ, B. (1966), 'Main Concepts in the Analysis of the Social Implications of Technical Change', in Hoselitz and Moore (1966).

HOSELITZ, B. and MOORE, W. (eds) (1966), *Industrialization and Society*, UNESCO, Mouton.

HUXLEY, A. (1969), *Brave New World*, Harmondsworth, Penguin.

HYMAN, RICHARD (1972), *Strikes*, Fontana, London.

INKELES, A. (1964), *What is Sociology?*, Englewood Cliffs, NJ, Prentice-Hall.

IRVINE, JOHN, MILES, IAN and EVANS, GEOFF (eds) (1979), *Demystifying Social Statistics*, London, Pluto Press.

JACKSON, B. and MARSDEN, D. (1969), *Education and the Working Class*, Harmondsworth, Penguin.

JALEE, P. (1970), *The Pillage of the Third World*, London, Monthly Review Press.

JOHNSTON, T. (1929), *A History of the Working Classes in Scotland*, Glasgow, Forward Publishing Co.

KARDINER, A. (ed.) (1963), *Psychological Frontiers of Scoiety*, New York, Columbia University Press.

KLEIN, V. (1960), *Working Wives*, London, Institute of Personnel Management Occasional Papers, no. 15.

KUHN, ANNETTE and WOLPE, ANNE MARIE (eds) (1978), *Feminism and Materialism*, London, Routlege & Kegan Paul.

LAZARSFELD, P. and THIELENS, W. (1955), *The Academic Mind*, Chicago, Free Press.

LEFEBVRE, H. (1968), *The Sociology of Marx*, London, Allen Lane, The Penguin Press.

LERNER, D. (1965), *The Passing of Traditional Society*, London, Free Press.

LESSNOFF, M. (1968), 'Parsons' System Problems', *Sociological Review*, vol. 16 (2), pp. 185–215.

LIDDINGTON, JILL and NORRIS, JILL (1978), *With One Hand Tied Behind Us*, London, Virago.

LINDESMITH, A. and STRAUSS, A. (1950), 'A Critique of Culture-Personality Writings', *American Sociological Review*, vol. 15, pp. 587–600.

LINTON, R. (1961), *The Cultural Background of Personality*, London, Routledge & Kegan Paul.

LIPSET, S. and SMELSER, N. (1961), 'Change and Controversy in Recent American Sociology', *British Journal of Sociology*, vol. XII (2), pp. 41–51.

LOCKWOOD, D. (1966), *The Blackcoated Worker*, London, Allen & Unwin.

LYND, R. (1969), *Knowledge for What?*, Princeton University Press.

MCCLELLAND, D. (1976), *The Achieving Society*, London, Halstead.

MACINTOSH, M. (1968), 'The Homosexual Role', *Social Problems*, vol. 16 (2), pp. 182–92.

MACINTYRE, A. (1967), *A Short History of Ethics*, London, Routledge & Kegan Paul.

MACINTYRE, A. (1969), *New Trends in Sociological Theory*, paper given to BSA Teachers' Section Conference, LSE, January, 1969.

MCKENZIE, R. and SILVER, A. (1968), *Angels in Marble*, London, Heinemann.

MACKIE, LINDSAY and PATTULLO, POLLY (1977), *Women at Work*, London, Tavistock.

MAGDOFF, HARRY (1969), *The Age of Imperialism*, London, Monthly Review Press.

MALINOWSKI, B. (1944), *A Scientific Theory of Culture*, Chapel Hill, University of North Carolina Press.

MALINOWSKI, B. (1961), *Argonauts of the Western Pacific*, London, Dutton.

MANDEL, E. (1968), 'The Lessons of May, 1968', *New Left Review*, no. 52, pp. 9–32.

MANDEL, E. (1972), *Marxist Economic Theory*, London, Merlin Press.

MANDEL, E. (1975), *Late Capitalism*, London, Monthly Review Press.

MANDEL, WILLIAM (1975), *Soviet Woman*, New York, Anchor Books.

MANNHEIM, K. (1966), *Ideology and Utopia*, London, Routledge & Kegan Paul.

MARCUSE, H. (1968a), *Reason and Revolution*, London, Routledge & Kegan Paul.

MARCUSE, H. (1968b), *Soviet Marxism*, London, Routledge & Kegan Paul.

MARCUSE, H. (1972), *One-Dimensional Man*, London, Sphere.

MARTIN, D. (1977), *Battered Wives*, New York, Pocket Books.

MARX, K. (1968), *The Civil War in France* and *The 18th Brumaire of Louis Napoleon*, in Marx and Engels (1968).

MARX, K. and ENGELS, F. (1968), *Selected Works*, London, Lawrence & Wishart.

MAYO, E. (1975), *The Social Problems of an Industrial Civilization*, London, Routledge & Kegan Paul.

MEAD, G. (1968), *Mind, Self and Society*, University of Chicago Press.

MEAD, M. (1978), *Sex and Temperament in Three Primitive Societies*, London, Routledge & Kegan Paul.

MERRINGTON, J. (1968), *Theory and Practice in Gramsci's Marxism*, in Miliband and Saville (1968).

MERTON, R. (1964), *Social Theory and Social Structure*, London, Collier-Macmillan.

MERTON, R. (1964), 'The Role Set: Problems in Sociological Theory', in Coser and Rosenberg (1964).

MESZAROS, ISTVAN (ed.) (1971), *Aspects of History and Class Consciousness*, London, Routledge & Kegan Paul.

MILIBAND, R. (1973), *The State in Capitalist Society*, London, Quartet Books.

MILIBAND, R. and SAVILLE, J. (eds) (1967), *Socialist Register, 1967*, London, Merlin Press.

MILIBAND, R. and SAVILLE, J. (eds) (1968), *Socialist Register, 1968*, London, Merlin Press.

MILL, J. (1961), *Auguste Comte and Positivism*, University of Michigan Press.

MILLETT, KATE (1971), *Sexual Politics*, New York, Avon.

MILLS, C. (1959a), *The Causes of World War III*, London, Secker & Warburg.

MILLS, C. (1959b), *The Power Elite*, New York, Oxford University Press.

MILLS, C. (ed.) (1967), *Images of Man*, New York, George Braziller.

MILLS, C. (ed.) (1969), *The Marxists*, Harmondsworth, Penguin.

MILLS, C. (1970), *The Sociological Imagination*, Harmondsworth, Penguin.

MITCHELL, J. (1971), *Women's Estate*, Harmondsworth, Penguin.

MOORE, B. (1963), 'Strategy in Social Science', in Stein and Vidich (1963).

MUSGRAVE, P. (1967), 'Towards a Sociological Theory of Occupational Choice', *Sociological Review*, vol. 15 (1), pp. 33–46.

MUSGROVE, F. and TAYLOR, P. (1969), *Society and the Teacher's Role*, London, Routledge & Kegan Paul.

MYRDAL, G. (1962), *Value in Social Theory*, London, Routledge & Kegan Paul.

NADEL, S. (1969), *The Theory of Social Structure*, London, Routledge & Kegan Paul.

NEUMANN, F. (1967), *Behemoth — The Structure and Practice of National Socialism*, London, Frank Cass.

NICLAUS, M. (1978) in Blackburn (1978).

NISBET, R. (1970), *The Sociological Tradition*, London, Heinemann.

NOVACK, G. (1968), 'Positivism and Marxism in Sociology', *International Socialist Review*, vol. 29 (4), pp. 27–37.

OBERG, K. (1961), 'The Kingdom of Ankole in Uganda', in Fortes and Evans-Pritchard (1961).

O'FAOLAIN, JULIA and MARTINES, LAURA (1974), *Not in God's Image*, London, Fontana.

ORLANSKY, H. (1949), 'Infant Care and Personality', *Psychological Bulletin*, vol. 46.

ORWELL, G. (1970), *Nineteen Eighty-Four*, Harmondsworth, Penguin.

OSSOWSKI, S. (1962), 'Empirical Sociology and Inner Experience', *Polish Sociological Bulletin*, vol. 2 (3–4), pp. 5–14.

OSSOWSKI, S. (1963), *Class Structure in the Social Consciousness*, London, Routledge & Kegan Paul.

OWEN, ROGER and SUTCLIFFE, BOB (eds) (1972), *Studies in the*

Theory of Imperialism, London, Longman.
PALLISTER, H. (1938), 'Vocational Preferences of School Leavers in a Scottish Industrial Area', *British Journal of Psychology,* vol. XXIX, pp. 144–66.
PARSONS, T. (1970), *The Social System,* London, Routledge & Kegan Paul.
PATEMAN, T. (ed.) (1972), *Counter Course,* Harmondsworth, Penguin.
PEARSON, GEOFFREY (1975), *The Deviant Imagination,* London, Macmillan.
PIAGET, J. (1953), *The Origin of Intelligence in the Child,* London, Routledge & Kegan Paul.
PIERCY, MARGE (1979), *Woman on the Edge of Time,* London, Woman's Press.
POMIANOWSKI, J. (1959), 'Mass Culture: A Case History', *Polish Perspectives,* no. 19, pp. 35–46.
POPPER, K. (1960), *The Poverty of Historicism,* London, Routledge & Kegan Paul.
PORTER, CATHY (1976), *Fathers and Daughters,* London, Virago.
PRIETO, HELIOS (1974), *Chile, The Gorillas are amongst Us,* London, Pluto Press.
RADCLIFFE-BROWN, A. (1963), *Structure and Function in Primitive Society,* London, Routledge & Kegan Paul.
REX, J. (1970), *Key Problems of Sociological Theory,* London, Routledge & Kegan Paul.
RHODES, R. (1968), 'The Disguised Conservatism in Evolutionary Development Theory', *Science and Society,* vol. XXXII (4), pp. 383–412.
RHODES, ROBERT I. (ed.) (1970), *Imperialism and Underdevelopment,* London, Monthly Review Press.
RICH, ADRIENNE (1977), *Of Woman Born,* London, Virago.
RIDDELL, CAROL (1968), 'Social Self-Government in Yugoslavia', *British Journal of Sociology,* vol. XIX, pp. 47–75.
RIDDELL, CAROL (1972), 'Towards a Structuralist Sociology of Development?', *Sociology,* VI (1), pp. 89–96.
RIDDELL, CAROL (1978), 'Patriarchy Does Mean Something', *Wires,* Summer.
RODNEY, WALTER (1976), *How Europe Underdeveloped Africa,* London, Bogle-L'Ouverture Publications.
ROSE, E. *et al.* (1969), *Colour and Citizenship,* Oxford University Press.
ROSE, HILARY and ROSE, STEPHEN (1976a), *The Political Economy of Science,* London, Macmillan.
ROSE, HILARY and ROSE, STEPHEN (1976b), *The Radicalization of Science,* London, Macmillan.
ROSENTHAL, R. (1967), *Experiments or Effects in Behavioural Research,* London, Halstead.
RUNCIMAN, W. (1966), *Relative Deprivation and Social Justice,* London, Routledge & Kegan Paul.
SAMUEL, R. (1960), 'Dr. Abrams and the End of Politics', *New Left Review,* no. 5, pp. 2–9.
SEABROOK, JEREMY (1978), *What Went Wrong, Working People and*

the Ideals of the Labour Movement, London, Gollancz.

SEELEY, J. (1963), 'Social Science? Some Probative Problems', in Stein and Vidich (1963).

SHARPE, SUE (1976), *Just Like a Girl,* Harmondsworth, Penguin.

SHAW, MARTIN (1975), *Marxism and Social Science,* London, Pluto Press.

SILBERMAN, C. (1964), *Crisis in Black and White,* New York, Random House.

SMELSER, N. (1960), *Social Change in the Industrial Revolution,* London, Routledge & Kegan Paul.

SOSENSKY, I. (1964), 'The Problem of Quality in Relation to Some Issues of Social Change', in Zollschan and Hirsch (1964).

SPENCER, H. (1971), *Principles of Sociology, Vol. I,* London, Gregg International.

STEIN, M. and VIDICH, A. (eds) (1963), *Sociology on Trial,* Englewood Cliffs, NJ, Prentice-Hall.

TAWNEY, R. (1969), *Religion and the Rise of Capitalism,* Harmondsworth, Penguin.

TAYLOR, C. (1958), 'The Poverty of The Poverty of Historicism', *Universities and Left Review,* no. 4, pp. 77–8.

TAYLOR, L. and TAYLOR, I. (1968), 'We Are All Deviationists Now – Some Comments on Crime', *International Socialism,* no. 34, pp. 29–32.

THERBORN, G. (1968), 'From Petrograd to Saigon', *New Left Review,* no. 48, pp. 3–11.

THOMPSON, E. (1970), *The Making of the English Working Class,* Harmondsworth, Penguin.

TROTSKY, L. (1975), *My Life,* Harmondsworth, Penguin.

VENESS, T. (1962), *School Leavers: Their Aspirations and Expectations,* London, Methuen.

WALKER, MARTIN (1976), *The National Front,* Harmondsworth, Penguin.

WEBB, J. (1962), 'The Sociology of a School', *British Journal of Sociology,* vol. XII (3), pp. 264–72.

WEBER, M. (1977), *The Protestant Ethic and the Spirit of Capitalism,* London, Allen & Unwin.

WESTERGAARD, JOHN and RESLER, HENRIETTA (1976), *Class in a Capitalist Society,* Harmondsworth, Penguin.

WHYTE, L. (1949), *The Science of Culture,* New York, Grove Press.

WILSON, AMRIT (1978), *Finding a Voice,* London, Virago.

WILSON, ELIZABETH (1977), *Women and the Welfare State,* London, Tavistock.

WOOLF, VIRGINIA (1977), *Three Guineas,* Harmondsworth, Penguin.

WORLD HEALTH ORGANIZATION (1966), *Aspects of Family Mental Health in Europe,* London, HMSO, Public Health Papers.

WORSLEY, P. (1957), 'Margaret Mead, Science or Science Fiction', *Science and Society,* vol. XXI (2).

WORSLEY, P. (1968), *The Trumpet Shall Sound,* London, Schocken.

WRONG, D. (1964), 'The Oversocialized Conception of Man in Modern Sociology', in Coser and Rosenberg (1964).

YOUNG, ROBERT (1973), 'The Human Limits of Nature', in Jonathan Benthall (ed.), *The Limits of Human Nature*, London, Allen Lane.

ZOLLSCHAN, G. and HIRSCH, W. (eds) (1964), *Explorations in Social Change*, London, Routledge & Kegan Paul.

ZOLLSCHAN, G. and PERUCCI, R. (1964), 'Social Stability and Social Progress: An Initial Presentation of Relevant Categories', in Zollschan and Hirsch (1964).